The House of the Prophet

The House of the Prophet

Devotion to Muhammad
in Islamic Mysticism

by
Claude Addas

Translated by
David Streight

FONS VITAE

First published in 2015 as
La Maison muhammadienne:
Aperçus de la dévotion au Prophète
en mystique musulmane
© Éditions Gallimard, Paris 2015
ISBN 2-07-014763-0

Published in 2024 by
Fons Vitae
49 Mockingbird Valley Drive
Louisville, KY 40207
http://www.fonsvitae.com

Copyright Fons Vitae 2024

Library of Congress Control Number: 2024934868

ISBN 978-1941610-985

This book was typeset by Neville Blakemore, Jr.

Printed in South Korea

To companions on the path
facing winds and tides

Contents

Introduction

Over a billion Muslims today call our planet home. Arabs, Persians, Asians, Africans...all worship the same God, all cherish the same Book. Yet the mental pictures of that one God vary considerably in the minds of these believers. Given such a diversity of images, rare is the person who can recognize Him in all of them: rare is the individual who can "embrace the totality of beliefs"[1]. Similarly diverse are the readings of the Book and the teachings that each reader takes from it. Rare also are minds capable of accepting all the meanings that the Divine Word brings – without rejecting any. The *umma*, the "Muslim Community" is of one voice. It is not however uniform; far from it. From one region to the next, from one culture to another, a multitude of differences – perhaps even divergences – may be seen.

There is nonetheless one thing shared by all who claim adherence to this Community – one thing that, beyond whatever ethnic, social, or cultural differences might be present – brings them together as one: it is their veneration of him whom Revelation proclaims to be a "mercy for the worlds [2]," he who by tradition has come to be known as *khayr al-anām*, "the best of created beings." In other words, between the image of the Prophet forged by Christianity – one still lingering in the pages of schoolbooks, that of a stubborn lawmaker, a sly and crafty leader of men – and that of a luminous, compassionate individual abiding in the hearts of Muslim believers, there lies an abyss in the depths of which misunderstandings and altercations from time immemorial have taken root and grown, and which the wounds of History (crusades, colonial conquests) have insidiously morphed into venomous resentment.

In a short book written as a commentary on (after several others) forty hadiths [3] ("Sayings" of the Prophet), Ibn Arabī's chosen disciple Qūnāwī recounted a dream he had one night in 1258:

> I saw the Prophet (Peace be upon him) wrapped in a shroud, stretched out on a litter. A few men were busy attaching him to it; his head was uncovered and his hair nearly touched the

ground. I said to them, "So what are you doing?" "He is dead," they replied, "and we want to take him to be buried." In my heart, I knew he was not dead, so I said "His face does not look to me like the face of a dead man; wait until we are certain of the fact." I leaned down close to his mouth and nose and discovered that he was breathing still, though his breath was faint. I called to the men and forbade them from pursuing their task. I then woke up, horrified and overwhelmed. Based on other experiences of this type, I grasped the symbolism: something serious was about to take place for Islam [4].

A dreadful dream, in truth. But not not as dreadful, as Qūnāwī would later learn, as the massacres perpetrated late that same night by Mongol hordes swarming into Baghdad. Islam only narrowly survived this wave. Foreboding dreams are not really the domain of historians, but this particular dream did carry an essential truth: to the Muslim mind, the Prophet is much more than the founder of the *umma*, he is its very soul. And from this perspective, Qūnāwī's account and the experience he relates are in no way exceptional: in the Muslim mind, a "vision of the Prophet in a dream" (*ru'yat al-nabī*) is by all means perceived as a grace, though a banal grace, if I may use that term, because anyone can hope for the experience and have those hopes fulfilled, even without a life of rigorous asceticism. Accounts of such events have been heard from the dawn of Islam to the present day, not only in the lives of the saints (*vitae sanctorum*), of course, but also in stories about individuals who in no way stand out religiously, socially, or intellectually from the masses. In short, we are talking about ordinary believers.

We should not really find this surprising. Called to turn five times a day toward the Ka'ba, the House of God, for ritual prayer (*salāt*), believers are also required – on several occasions during each time of prayer – to directly address God's Messenger. They are called to exclaim "May Peace be upon you, o Prophet...!," with the assurance that their invisible interlocutor will both hear them and respond: he is both alive and engaged with them [5].

This mysterious dialogue between the praying believer and the Prophet that is so much a part of the ritual prayer punctuating the daily life of believers points out something fundamental about Islam in the lives of hundreds of millions of Muslims throughout the world – in Africa as well as Asia, from East to West. It is a trait to keep in mind in any attempt to decipher the mindsets or behaviors of Muslim societies: when Muhammad took his last breath, in 632, his passing did mark the end of his terrestrial existence, but at least in the eyes of his religious followers, that death did not break the indissoluble bond which, beyond time and space, kept him tied to his community. And what is even more important to understand is that this bond, transcending differences in culture, language, ethnicity, and era, is a bond of *mutual love.*

We are touching, here, on a fundamental fact of Islamic piety, broadly speaking. Not only is the religious and social behavior of those men and women who place their faith in Muhammad affected, but in a more general sense this fact is foundational to their cultural heritage. After all, we should not forget that the "profession of faith," the *shahāda* upon which being a Muslim is based, requires both belief in a single God and, just as categorically, it requires bearing witness to the authenticity of the Prophet's Mission.

A number of easily observable phenomena – both past and present, and from all levels of society – provide evidence of the strong devotion Muslims hold for the Prophet. One example of this can be seen in the widespread distribution of an entire branch of devotional literature focusing on the "merits of the Prophet." Some of these works are quite short, others are voluminous; some are prose and some in verse; in every language of the Islamic world, they all extol the unequalled perfection of the Prophet [6]. Though the first examples of this type of writing appeared in the third century after the *hijra*, the genre truly came into its own in the sixth century, when Qāḍī ʿIyāḍ (d. 544/1149) penned his famous *Shifāʾ*. The editorial success of these regularly reprinted works (they can easily be downloaded today, from countless sites, from the Internet) more than suggests their appeal to a broad readership.

Just as impressive is the huge popularity of works that list the many sentences and phrases used as invocations to the Prophet, each of which is reputed to have some efficacious property, especially those purporting to bring about dreams that include a vision of God's Chosen One. Shortly before the fratricidal war that would soon lay waste to his country broke out, a famous shaykh from Damascus made a pronouncement on the subject at a highly publicized public conference: "There is not a single Muslim who does not wish to see the Prophet in a dream." Let us add to the hyperbole: for the huge majority of Muslims – wealthy or impoverished, erudite or illiterate, speakers of Arabic or not – the Prophet, far from the intransigent lawmaker and warlord whose image so worries the West, is seen more than anything as a vehicle for divine mercy, the *ghawth*, "he who comes to their aide." We have only to reflect for a moment on the abject misery and the immense suffering endured by so many who are born and die in underprivileged lands for the tremendous importance of this aspect of devotion to the Prophet to become easier to understand.

The celebration of the Prophet's *mawlid*, his birth, which tended to become popular in the 13th century, is another of the many visible signs of devotion to the Prophet, and an indication of his ever increasing importance, over the years, in the daily lives of Muslims. The festivities and various devotional practices that arose to mark his birthday – gatherings for *samaʿ* ("spiritual concerts"), collective recitation of prayers composed in the Prophet's honor, songs, poems – as well as the strong outpouring of emotion accompanying these events were clearly not unanimously approved of by the ulama [7]. Regardless of the period in time, there have always been those who disparaged these practices, albeit without success.

Love for the Prophet abides in the hearts of believers. It is from here that they draw the power of hope, against winds and tides. The angrier the storm, the more their fervor grows. Indifferent to the occasional demands for order by stern jurists offended by these (sometimes boisterous) demonstrations of affection, their love rings out loud and clear. A number of them – actually, the majority – would never have the financial means to travel to the Holy Sites, and thus to pay homage at the tomb of God's Messenger. Assured that borders in neither time nor space would get in the way of his affection for them, they take solace in repeating the famous words where the Prophet is said to have been announcing his imminent death: "I would have loved to meet my brothers!" "Are we then not your brothers?," asked the companions who were present with him. "You are my companions. *My brothers are those who believe in me without having seen me*"[8].

Seen as "the best of created beings" – or, to use the time-honored expression of Muslim mystics, "the Perfect Man" (*al-insān al-kāmil*) – the Prophet is also considered the paragon of spiritual excellence. Thus the imperative regarding the very idea of the search for God in Islam, that the prophetic model be imitated: there is no hope of reaching the threshold of the Divine Presence – that is, no hope of attaining sainthood (*walāya*) – without resolute and humble conformity to the perfect model incarnated by Muhammad. This conformity, being a question of mystical tradition, cannot be reduced to a pure formality. It clearly implies strict observance of a variety of religious obligations and thus is seen, essentially, as adherence to – as "attachment" to (*ta'alluq*) in the strongest sense of the word – the Prophet's very being, to the point that he dwells within one. We are no longer on a doctrinal plane here, but rather at the level of experience, of "feeling." Sent to "all of humanity," [9] as the Qur'an declares, Muhammad is, all the more so, for each of them, *within* each of them: "And know that God's messenger is within you" [10] states a verse of Revelation that Muslim spiritual seekers take literally as they strive to embody its deep meaning. From a perspective like this, the Prophet is not revered just for being God's Messenger to the universe; he is revered because he has taken on the role of "spiritual guide" (*murshid*) for those who embark on the perilous journey toward the "Lord of the worlds," and without whose assistance they are destined to wander indefinitely. Just as the Ka'ba is the *qibla*, the direction that believers face physically when they engage in ritual prayer, so also is the Prophet the *qibla* toward whom the hearts of those wishing a glimpse of the Eternal turn: he is the pole star that never ceases to shine through the depths of night.

Let us be quite clear: this is not a subsidiary issue, and even less so is it something out of folklore. Rather, it is foundational to Islamic mysticism. "Attachment to the Prophet" – an expression found increasingly in documents dealing with mysticism as the centuries unfold – does not represent one path toward spiritual realization among others. In the view of Muslim spiritual thinkers, it is the one and only route of access to sainthood. This "prophetocentrism" so characteristic of the concept of *itinerarium in Deum* in Islam can be seen as early as the first generations of mystics. Throughout the history of Sufism, though, it has undergone modifications, minor adjustments in formulation as well as in the devotional practices of which it was the source. The preponderant place it started to take in the teachings of Sufi masters from the 18th century on, as well as in the rituals of their brotherhoods, has also been the subject of debate among scholars in recent decades.

The deep veneration held for the Prophet in Muslim societies – a reverence that left its mark on a number of both individual and collective behaviors in Muslim society as a whole – has, as a matter of fact, long drawn the attention of ethnologists, sociologists, and scholars of Islam. Popular manifestations of this devotion have been the subject of countless publications, and even of travel accounts. One sign of this is Annemarie Schimmel's impressive (though not exhaustive, and already dated) bibliography [11]. Recent studies have continued to make valuable contributions to her research [12]. Outside the circle of specialists, some of the more extreme forms that love for the Prophet can take (with less scrupulous individuals sometimes pulling the strings) have grabbed the attention of a broader public; the "Rushdie Affair" and cartoon caricatures of the Prophet are but two examples.

Among the many works dedicated to this major aspect of Muslim piety – besides Tor Andrae's pioneering 1918 book [13] – Schimmel's *And Muhammad Is His Messenger* deserves special mention. Schimmel explores the "veneration of the Prophet" motif in the "poetry of Islamic peoples," meaning the majority of the languages spoken in the Islamic world. The work is thus not only of immense value, it is also food for serious thought. It does not touch on every aspect of the question, however, by far; nor does it pretend to do so. Schimmel's long familiarity with Muslim literature broadly speaking, and with Muslims themselves, led to the German scholar's observation that the figure of the Prophet is omnipresent in Islamic piety – throughout the ages and in every corner of the Muslim world. It just had to be confirmed, and that is what she did.

But "worship of the Prophet" raises other questions, starting with these: why such reverence for someone Revelation refers to categorically as nothing more than a "human" like others? By way of analogy with the adoration of Mary in Christianity, the word *hyperdulia* may be appropriate, but not *latria*. Where do Muslim believers get their certainty that Muhammad is not only the last of God's messengers, but that he is also *sayyid al-mursalīn*, the "chief Messenger" (to use one of the many honorific names tradition has given him) and that his magisterium – his position of spiritual and lawgiving authority – therefore has something unique and exceptional about it? Did this originate in early Islam, or is it more a case of some rogue "popular belief" that the passage of time allowed to be grafted onto more common teachings? What specific forms and functions did this veneration for the Prophet take on within the mystical tradition?

The early chapters (1 - 4) of this book will examine the doctrinal issues behind this extraordinary devotion. I will address the decisive role played by Sufi teachers, especially the one whose disciples referred to as "the greatest teacher," or "the greatest master," Ibn Arabī (d. 638/1240). As a matter of fact it was he who, in countless writings but especially in his wide-ranging mystical summa, the *Futūhāt Makkiyah* (The Illuminations of Mecca), gave structure to a doctrine of prophetology that previously was seen only in brief and disparate pronouncements in mystical literature. It was Ibn Arabī also who managed to delineate, in precise terms, the main elements of this doctrine. More than anything, it is to him that the doctrine's universality is due. The idea of the universality of the Prophet's spiritual authority may be argued, but the Shaykh al-Akbar's influence on how the Muslim world comes to understand the figure of the Prophet cannot be denied.

In a second set of chapters (5, 6, and 7), I will look into the role this devotion to the Prophet plays – and the importance it has – for Muslim spiritual seekers in the course of spiritual development. In so doing I will focus especially on a short treatise by one of Ibn Arabī's later disciples, 'Abd al-Karīm al-Jīlī (d. 811/1409). In my opinion, this little work has had a decisive influence on both the spread and the increasing popularity of devotional practices related to "attachment to the Prophet," especially among the reformational teachers of the 18th century.

Finally, in closing this overview of the most basic aspects of devotion to the Prophet, the idea of *ahl al-bayt* must be addressed. Strictly speaking, the term refers to Muhammad's family and his descendants. Veneration of the Prophet's family is common among both Sunnis and Shi'ites. But it is a source of discord at the same time, to the extent that, for the latter, other specific attributes are taken for granted, especially where the delicate question of temporal power and who holds it is concerned. Regardless of what people might think, Ibn Arabī had no particular sympathy for Shi'ism, and he did not share this view. The interpretation he proposed for the concept of "House of the Prophet" highlights the key role it was called to play in fulfilling the Prophet's role in salvation. For this reason my short plunge into the depths of Islamic mysticism will conclude, as it began, in the company of the Shaykh al-Akbar.

Notes
---

[1] IBN ARABĪ, 1911, II, pp. 220.

[2] Qur'an 21:107.

[3] Sadr al-Dīn Qūnāwī (d. 672/1274) died before finishing his commentary, which addresses only twenty-nine hadiths.

[4] QŪNĀWĪ, 1990, pp. 127-128.
[5] Cf. ABŪ DĀWŪD, 1998, "manāsik," 96, II, pp. 539-540.
[6] SCHIMMEL, 1984, ch II.
[7] In passing, let us recognize – and salute – the courage of Saudi Ibn ʿAlawī (d. 2004), who, for supporting the orthodox nature of the *mawlid* celebration (cf. *al-Dhakhāʾir al-muhammadiyya*, Cairo, n.d.), became subject to a broad smear campaign in Saudi Arabia, beginning in the 1980s. The authorities called for his public repentance, but Ibn ʿAlawī refused to comply and was consequently relieved of his duties as professor at his university in Mecca. After the September 11 tragedy, Ibn ʿAlawī was nevertheless forgiven and his reputation restored by the Saudi regime (on this subject, cf. KATZ, 2007, pp. 184-187, 193-194, 215).
[8] IBN HANBAL, 1995-2001, "Musnad Anas b. Mālik," XX, p. 38, num. 12579; WENSINCK, 1936-1969, VII, p. 166. This hadith may be compared to John 20:29.
[9] Qurʾan 34:28.
[10] Qurʾan 49:7.
[11] SCHIMMEL, 1984, pp. 314-341.
[12] Cf. especially M. H. Katz's remarkable study of the *mawlid* (KATZ, 2007); KAPTEIN, 1993; HOFFMAN, 1992; MEIER, 1999 (a).
[13] ANDRAE, 1918.

Chapter One

"The Prophet is nearer to believers than they are to their own souls" [1]

"MY LORD IS MY NOURISHMENT..."

"Say: I am but a man (*bashar*) like you...[2]." The Prophet receives this command from God three different times in the Qur'an. Deciphering its meaning was not overly difficult for exegetes, nor did it require long dissertations: as "chosen" as he may have been, they pointed out, Muhammad is but a simple mortal; not an angel, not a god, not even a demi-god [3].

Given writers who tend toward verbosity, might the terseness of the Qur'an's injunction not preclude any possibility of confusion? It might be fair to wonder if this solemn assertion of the Prophet's *bashariyya* – his membership in the "human race" – might include both a warning against attempts to deify him, and consequently an implicit reference to Christian teachings about the nature of Christ. There is nothing to keep us from entertaining the thought. Ibn Arabī, who mentions this verse and subtly develops its meaning through a number of passages in his book, does not hesitate to make the comparison [4].

This does however present a paradox. In thus highlighting, three times, the *bashariyya* of God's Messenger – and thereby also highlighting the humility (in the etymological sense of the term) inherent in the human condition – Revelation diminishes the importance of the very individual who was chosen above all others to be its recipient – the very one who, in fact, in so many other verses, it raises up. It is precisely upon this theme of the Prophet's *bashariyya*, moreover, that the invective of Muhammad's enemies was so focused as they pointed out his failure to transcend the everyday human condition: "he eats and goes to the market" [5]. In this case, God is on their side, yet elsewhere He also proclaims: "In truth, you

17

are of a sublime nature" [6]. It might be added in passing that the hadith literature shows this same ambiguity, with the Prophet in one place declaring "I am but a man who gets angry as others do" [7] while affirming elsewhere – in regard to his practice of continual fasting – "I am not like you, I spend the night in the presence of my Lord, who is my nourishment and slakes my thirst" [8].

Before attempting to explain this paradox, a closer look at the concept of *bashariyya* is in order; it plays an important role in the issue of Islamic prophetology, and does so in a number of ways. The word *bashar* appears several times in the Qur'an. Sometimes it is in reference to the human species in general [9] – it has this meaning in Sura 74, where it is used four times – and even more frequently it refers to particular human beings, regardless of how many there are, or what their gender is. In all cases it goes without saying that the "man" referred to is a man of *flesh*, and thus mortal. The primary meaning of the word *bashar* is, in fact, "flesh, epidermis," and the idea of being "of the flesh" is inherent in current uses of the word. As such, this distinguishes the word *bashar* from the word *insān*, which also means "man," but in a more abstract sense. It is remarkable, by the way, that in the two Suras mentioning the Annunciation, when Mary replies to the Angel, "How could I be with child when no man has touched me?" [10], she uses the word *bashar* – thus specifically denoting a being of flesh and blood. *Bashar* actually shows up often in the Qur'an to differentiate between the human race and the angels, *malak* [11]: carnal beings versus spiritual beings.

Bashar thus refers to man in the sense of what is most humble and perishable about him: his plasticity, destined for decrepitude. In accord with his original status as *imago Dei*, his vulnerability itself makes any possibility of theomorphism unimaginable. Thus the tragic errors, starting with Satan, who was mistaken about Adam's low provenance [12]: summoned by God to prostrate himself before the first man, he categorically refused: "I am not about to prostrate myself before a man (*bashar*) that You created out of clay" [13]. And the mistake made by those who found themselves incapable of transcending appearances; their "eyes of flesh" could discern only the bodily forms of the messengers before them, sent by God. "You are nothing but men, like us," they repeated, time after time [14]. And those demanding miracles they could witness with their own eyes [15] (thus, on the physical plane), so powerless they were to perceive *ghayb* – that which belongs to the realm of the strictly metaphysical and thus eludes the world of forms.

Since it deals specifically with Muhammad's apostolic mission, it might be noted that Revelation somewhat takes the initiative here, proclaiming from the outset that the Prophet belongs to the human race. That, in and of itself, implies that the Prophet – regardless of how "sublime" [16] his nature might be – is still only a creature. And, it would be wrong to replace the error of only taking his outer form into consideration (the part that makes him a member of the human race) with a mistake no less serious: that of denying his *bashariyya*, his "humanity" – for this would lead, ineluctably, to idolatry.

It is moreover remarkable that in the three verses addressing Muhammad's *bashariyya*, each time it is because God demands – using the imperative mood, "Say!" (*qul*) – that the Prophet declare his equality to everyone else: as a simple mortal. Lowered "to the lowest of the low" [17], Muhammad proclaims his *faqr* – that "indigence" so inherent in the status of man, of which his decomposable body is the most obvious evidence – only when God makes him do so.

In any case, the Qur'an does more than just suggest that the Prophet is a "man," fully endowed with all the instability and limitation that accompany the human condition: he argues about his status as a husband and head of a family, he mentions certain marital problems he was required to deal with, he announces his inevitable death, never to return. And what about all the quite sizable collections of hadiths that, in passing along the Sunna – the sayings, actions, and "customs" of the Prophet – offer intimate glimpses into his daily life, from how he drank or ate, to even how he smiled? Revelation never says he was a superman. Quite the contrary, because throughout his life he fully actualized his condition as *bashar*, along with all that this condition implied in terms of servitude; because he was presented as the "model par excellence" [18], and because, for fourteen centuries now, his Community has never failed to be nurtured by his example.

As a matter of fact, instead of diminishing his prestige in the eyes of his followers, the way Revelation "exposed" the Prophet's *bashariyya* has only helped to increase devotion to him, in the sense that it allows believers to see themselves in him. After all, he was a man who experienced both the delight of holding a loved one in his arms and the pain of burying the bodies of kin. In short, he was a man steeped in the earthly joys and suffering that punctuate life for all mortal beings.

That the Prophet is a "man" is not the only point that Revelation makes; it also affirms that, *in this regard*, he is identical to his fellow human beings: "I am no more than a man, *like* [19] you (*mithlukum*)." This characteristic establishes a bond of solidarity between God's Messenger and his *umma*. It informs believers that God's Chosen One experienced normal human aches and pains to the same extent that they do. This was true both for the pains he endured because of his physical vulnerabilities and for those arising out of his innate disposition. In regard to the former, Ibn Arabī reminds – in reference to the verse just quoted – that the Prophet felt such pain from hunger at one point that he set stones on his stomach [20]; and for the latter, we have the hadith mentioned above: "I am but a human being, like you; I get angry like other men and I satisfy my needs as they do." Reference to the average mortal being is a clear indication, the author of the *Futūhāt* notes, that this is not about anger and satisfaction "for God's benefit" (*li Llāh*) – a spiritual attitude out of desire to see divine rights respected – but rather "for the benefit of oneself or others" [21], meaning that these are natural inclinations emanating from the animal soul [22]. Ibn Arabī mentions at the same time that being exempt in the physical world from characteristics inherent in human nature is a gift granted to no mortal being [23]; it is however possible to sanctify these innate tendencies.

And this was precisely one of the duties that fell upon the Prophet: that of showing his fellow human beings how to achieve this sanctification. We learn this from a hadith that Ibn Arabī wrote a long commentary on: God's Messenger states, "I have been called to perfect the noble characters (*makārim al-akhlāq*)" [24]. As Ibn Arabī explains, not a single character trait has been written in man that does not have its point of departure in the divine – and which, therefore is noble in its essence [25]. Anything vile or blameworthy that it might appear to be covering over is purely incidental (*'aradī*) [26] and due to its being manifested at an inappropriate moment.

By virtue of being the "model par excellence" – which is exactly what the Sunna *is*, "saintly behavior" – the role of God's Messenger also includes showing that each and every character trait can, and should, be reinvested with the noble status already intrinsic in it – provided that the manifestation of that character trait is subordinated to the observance of Divine Law, the *sharīʿa*, in the broader sense of the term (i.e., the "ensemble of rules instituted by God"). The Qurʾan – Revelation in its most definitive form – is our reminder of this Law in its "Book" (*kitāb*) form, while the Prophet – who incarnates practice of the Law – represents It in the form of a man [27]. Seen in this way, it is easy to see how "imitation" of the Prophet as "model" might lead to the fulfillment of "theosis" (*tahaqquq bi akhlāqi Llāh*) [28].

From this perspective, rather than slipping by almost unnoticed, the *bashariyya* of God's Prophet, which Revelation proclaims loud and clear, is a proclamation of "good news" (*bushra*) [29] for believers, in its showing that there is nothing in man that by its nature presents an obstacle to his perfection – or better said, that presents an obstacle to the restoration of his original perfection [30]. The Prophet was not a god who took on human characteristics. He was a human being in his entirety, one who actualized his status as *imago Dei* through every constituent element of his being – a status granted by God to this particular man, and by virtue of which he was singled out to be His *khalīfa*, His "representative" on earth. He is evidence of the fact that theomorphosis is not concerned with *zāhir* (that which is "apparent") any less than it is with *bātin* (that which is "hidden"), and that everything in man, *including everything related to his carnality*, both can and should be associated with the process of sanctification, for without this there would be no possibility of palingenesis, of full and complete restoration of man's original nature.

Besides, it is in his very composition as a being of body and flesh, according to Ibn Arabī, that man is superior to other creatures [31]. As he explains, God gave man the name *bashar* "for having created him 'by direct contact' (*mubāsharatan*) [32], with His own hands, unassisted, in the manner His Majesty wished" [33]. This privilege has been granted to no other creature: "Thus, man is superior to the other creatures only by virtue of his being a human being fashioned from clay (*basharan min tīn*)" [34]. Whence the reply to Satan, "What kept you from prostrating yourself before that which *I created with My own hands*" [35]? The human being is noble because He Who created him is Noble.

"MY EYES SLEEP, BUT MY HEART DOES NOT"

It would be incorrect to conclude from the above that, in their devotion to the Prophet, Muslims revere only the individual that the Prophet *was* at a certain time and place, as *bashar* – exceptional though he was, in their eyes. As significant as this aspect of devotion to him was, it pales in comparison to the spiritual preeminence that the faithful see him having in the spiritual hierarchy, on the one hand, and to the role of intercessor that Tradition has attributed to him, on the other. These two characteristics are in fact tightly interlinked: it is because of his unsurpassable perfection that the Prophet is in the best position to intercede with God on behalf of men. Whence the practice, seen as widely today as in the past, of *istighātha*, the "plea for succor" that believers address to him whenever circumstances present the need [36]. If there truly is a conviction that nurtures hope in believers and bolsters their faith, it is the certainty that – despite his physical absence since the time of his interment – God's Messenger is still very much *alive* and *close* to them [37].

We are not dealing with an issue of "popular belief" here. Rather, this is an article of faith held by most Muslims [38], from the least educated to the most erudite. It has its basis in the Qur'an – "The Messenger of God is nearer to believers than they are to their own souls" [39] – as well as in hadith, where a number of traditions assert that the Prophet hears and responds to those asking that God's blessing might be upon him [40]. In this same regard, even Ibn Arabī mentions the statement attributed to the Prophet: "My eyes sleep, but my heart does not" [41]. Similarly, he notes that sleep – traditionally referred to as "the small death" – only affected Muhammad's corporal envelope, just as death only altered his physical constitution. His heart is, still, awake [42].

Beyond a substantial amount of popular literature consisting, most notably, of countless collections of reputedly effective [43] "prayers upon the Prophet," this faith in the unfailing spiritual presence of God's Chosen One has given birth to a curious epistolary genre called "Letters to the Prophet" (*rasā'il ilā l-nabī*). Maqqarī transcribed some of these pleas to God's Messenger in his *Nafh al-tīb*, most notably those where Ibn al-Khatīb (d. 776/1375) begs the Prophet to provide assistance to the kingdom of Granada, the last bastion of Muslim Spain [44].

Quite different is what led his Damascene contemporary, Taqī al-Dīn Subkī (d. 756/1355), to write requesting the Prophet's intercession. Worried about the increasing number of Ibn Taymiyya's partisans, he asked that the Prophet assure him of his right to counter the Hanbalī doctor's subversive ideas, in particular those dealing with *istighātha* [45]. In Ibn Taymiyya's view, the practice was evidence of "associationism" (*shirk*), which he wanted absolutely forbidden [46]. Convinced that his plea was heard, Subkī composed a short treatise showing the orthodoxy of *istighātha* [47].

Ibn al-Khatīb and Subkī were two of the most erudite among the ulama of their time [48]. Both held the position of qadi: until proven otherwise, considered "enlightened" men. Both were also staunch proponents not only of the idea that the Prophet is always present in his subtle mode (whence the *istighātha*), but also *that he existed even prior to the creation of the first man.*

Subkī and Ibn al-Khatīb are alike in their support for the idea of the preexistence of the Prophet, in line with a literal interpretation of the famous hadith, "I was a prophet (*kuntu nabiyyan*) when Adam was still between spirit and body" [49] or, according to a version of the same hadith that, in contrast, does not appear in the canonical collections: "between water and clay." This position is not overly surprising in Ibn al-Khatīb's case, given the considerable impression Sufism had on the development of his thought, as is clearly seen in his *Rawd al-ta'rīf.* It is however significant that he cites the alternate version of the hadith [50], since its validity was questioned by the Doctors of the Law, though authenticated by Ibn Arabī, who steadfastly preferred it [51] (a position for which Ibn Taymiyya refused to pardon him) [52].

In fact, the vehemence of the Hanbalī doctor's attack of the *Futūhāt*'s author regarding this specific point is all the more surprising since, when all is said and done, the two versions express the same idea. Ibn Taymiyya accepted the first version as valid; Subkī was not mistaken when, in opting for the version preferred by his colleagues, he also (in line with teachings of the Sufi masters) was aware of its evident meaning:

> It has been established that God created spirits prior to bodies. So his words "I was a prophet when Adam was still between spirit and body" may refer either to his noble spirit or to some reality (*haqīqa*) among (other, extrasensory) realities, since our intellects are incapable of knowing (extrasensory) realities. God alone

knows them, as do those whom He assists via divine light. [...] *Thus his reality was present from that moment on, even though his physical appearance did not appear until later.* [...] From this we know that those interpreting [this hadith] to mean that God knew he would be a prophet have not grasped its [true] meaning. [...] If its meaning was simply the knowledge that God had about his becoming a prophet, that would not constitute anything specific about the Prophet, since God knew about all the prophets who ended up being prophets [53].

Qastallānī (d. 923/1517), more than pleased by being able to have a scholar of impeccable orthodoxy to support his case [54], made considerable use of Subkī's testimony in his *Mawāhib laduniyya* [55]. Like Qāḍī ʿIyāḍ's *Shifāʾ*, the work was designed to prove the preeminence of the Prophet, and ended up contributing considerably to the literary spread of this theme across the Muslim world. According to him, Subkī's sights were actually on imam Ghazālī, a point he supports by a short work attributed to Ghazālī dealing with the creation of Adam. The attribution should nevertheless be looked at with caution; Ibn Arabī formally disagreed with it [56]. In his very helpful commentary on the *Mawāhib* [57], Zurqānī notes that the opinion according to which *kuntu nabiyyan*, "I was a prophet," referred solely to the fact that God knew from all eternity that Muhammad would be a prophet, was the prevailing opinion among many ulama, epecially Ibn Taymiyya. With his usual forcefulness Ibn Taymiyya claimed that, in this case, *kuntu* ("I was") is a synonym for *kutibtu* ("I was on the list") [58]; in other words, the only thing at issue here is *taqdīr*, that which God has decreed from all eternity [59], and not the actual fulfillment of the decree [60]. Subkī felt a moral duty to challenge the contentions of the man he considered a dangerous innovator, particularly those where the Prophet was concerned [61]. So under the circumstances it is quite probable that Ibn Taymiyya was the real target of his criticism.

Does it really matter? What we can see is that, even though he rejects the interpretation preferred by most of the ulama, the learned Shafi'ite did not go so far as to state explicitly in writing that he sided with the idea preached by masters of the Way. His choice of words is eloquent here: the word *haqīqa*, which he uses to refer to the mode of the Prophet's preexistence, includes a concept that is actually somewhat vague and thus susceptible to a variety of interpretations [62]. Much more meaningful is the expression *nūr muhammadī*, "the Light of Muhammad," which, in contrast to Ibn al-Khaṭīb [63], Subkī does not use; even if it goes back to the same idea, it has much stronger doctrinal connotations and – to the extent that it belongs to the terminology of an entire gnostic tradition in Islam, even being one of its key terms – it raises suspicions.

Notes

[1] Qurʾan 33:6.
[2] Qurʾan 18:110 and, worded differently, 17:93.
[3] Cf., for example, TABARĪ, n.d., VIII, 15th part, p. 109, VIII, 16th part, p. 31; NISĀBŪRĪ, n.d., VIII, 16th part, p. 25; QURTUBĪ, 1933-1950, VI, 11th part, p. 69, VIII, 15th part, p. 340.
[4] IBN ARABĪ, 1911, I, p. 664; Id., 1980, p. 141; ID., 210, p. 89. Qushayrī – in reference to verse 17:93 – cites verse 4:172, which states in reference to Jesus: "The Messiah does not disdain being the servant of God" (QUSHAYRĪ, 2000, II, p. 203). On other interpretations of this series of verses, cf. SULAMĪ, 2001, I, p. 317, II, pp. 215-216; HAQQĪ, n.d., V, pp. 204, 309; ʿAYN AL-QUDĀT, 1992, pp. 162-163, 223-224.
[5] Qurʾan, 25:7.
[6] Qurʾan, 68:4.
[7] Cf. MUSLIM, n.d., "*birr*," 95, vol. IV, p. 2012; several hadiths begin with the words "*innamā anā basharun*"; cf. WENSINCK, 1936-1969, I, p. 183.
[8] MUSLIM, n.d., "*siyām*," 55, 56, II, p. 774; cf. the interpretation offered by IBN ARABĪ, 1911, I, pp. 638, 658, III, p. 43.
[9] Let us remember that the expression *Abū l-bashar* refers to Adam as the father of the human race.
[10] Qurʾan, 3:47, 19:20; cf. Luke 1, 34.
[11] Qurʾan, 12:31, 17:94-95, 74: 29-31.
[12] It is precisely because he had perceived no more than Adam's external form that Satan is called "the Blind One" (cf. AWN, 1983, p. 90).
[13] Qurʾan 15:33.
[14] Qurʾan 11:27, 21:3, 23:24, 23:33, 26:154, 26:186, 36:15, 54:24, 64:6.
[15] Qurʾan 21:5, 17:94.
[16] Qurʾan 68:4.
[17] Qurʾan 95:5.
[18] Qurʾan 33:21.
[19] Italics mine.
[20] IBN ARABĪ, 1911, III, p. 23.
[21] *Ibid.*, I, p. 350, III, pp. 191, 337.
[22] *Ibid.*, II, pp. 108-109.
[23] *Ibid.*, p. 687.
[24] *Ibid.*, pp. 241-243, 562.
[25] *Ibid.*, p. 363.
[26] *Ibid.*, p. 562.

[27] *Ibid.*, p. 363, IV, p. 58. Whence the importance of the idea of "noble charac-ters" (*makārim al-akhlāq*) in Ibn Arabī's initiatory teachings, where adherence to the *sharīʿa* is a condition of access to the highest degrees of spiritual re-alization. It is nevertheless significant that to Tirmidhī's question "By what means did the Muhammadan Seal of Sanctity reach that [degree of sancti-ty]?" the *Futūhāt*'s author replied "by practicing noble character" (*ibid.*, II, pp. 49-50).
[28] Cf. CHODKIEWICZ, 1994 (b), pp. 201-226.
[29] The word has the same root as the word *bashar*.
[30] Najm al-Dīn Kubrā greatly expanded upon this doctrinal aspect of the Proph-et's *bashariyya* in the *tafsīr* attributed to him (cf. BALLANFAT, 2002, pp. 194-197). Cf. also HAQQĪ, n.d., III, p. 542.
[31] Nūr al-Dīn Isfarāyinī developed the same idea, especially asserting that *bashariyya* is a "cloak of honor" granted to man, thanks to which he can reach total perfection (cf. ISFARĀYINĪ, 1986, pp. 116-117, note 182).
[32] This word is also based on the root *b.sh.r.*
[33] IBN ARABĪ, 1911, II, p. 70; ID., 1980, pp. 144-145. We find the same interpreta-tion in Tirmidhī (cf. GOBILLOT, 1996, p. 88).
[34] IBN ARABĪ, 1980, p. 145.
[35] Qurʾan 38:75 (italics mine).
[36] On controversies relative to this practice, cf. NABHĀNĪ, 1996 (b), ch. II.
[37] On this subject, cf. SCHIMMEL, 1984, p. 92-94.
[38] "Most Muslims" in this case (does it even bear saying?) does not include the Wahhabīs and the doctrinal currents the movement has spurred. They ve-hemently oppose veneration of the saints and of the Prophet in its cultural aspects, like *istighātha*, which in their opinion is related to superstition, at best, and idolatry at worst.
[39] Qurʾan 33:6.
[40] NABHĀNĪ, 1966 (a), pp. 14-16, makes a list of these traditions (cf. also ID., 1997, pp. 77ff).
[41] Cf. WENSINCK, 1936-1969, V, p. 453.
[42] IBN ARABĪ, 1911, II, p. 108.
[43] Cf. SCHIMMEL, 1984, pp. 94-104; PADWICK, 1961, pp. 154-165, 222-225.
[44] Cf. MAQQARĪ, 1986, IX, pp. 80-104 (cf. also II, pp. 49ff, X, pp. 283-289).
[45] NABHĀNĪ, 1996 (b), pp. 132-133.
[46] MEMON, 1976, pp. 310-311 (English translation of IBN TAYMIYYA, n.d., I, 1st part, p. 12-13).
[47] SUBKĪ, 1996, pp. 56, 130, 104, 105, 132, etc.
[48] Ibn al-Khatīb's death was undoubtedly a tragic one, but his condemnation was less a consequence of his religious opinions than of his political difficul-ties.
[49] WENSINCK, 1936-1969, VI, p. 335.
[50] MAQQARĪ, 1986, IX, pp. 82, 85; IBN AL-KHATĪB, 1970, I, p. 158.
[51] Ibn Arabī was not the first, by far, to prefer the second version. Among writ-ers who preceded him were BIDLĪSĪ, 1999, p. 129; ʿAYN AL-QUDĀT, 1992, p. 162; and IBN QASĪ, 1997, pp. 364, 367.

[52] IBN TAYMIYYA, n.d., II, 4th part, p. 8.

[53] The treatise is titled *al-Ta'zim wa l-minna fī qawlihi...*; BROCKELMANN, 1937-1949, II, pp. 87-88 (Sup., II, pp. 102-104), mentions a manuscript in *Dār al-kutub*; see passages in QASTALLĀNĪ, 1996, I, pp. 72-74, 79-80, VIII, pp. 346-351; NABHĀNĪ, 1998, I, pp. 509ff. Italics mine.

[54] QASTALLĀNĪ, 1996, subscribes to the theory of the Prophet's preexistence, giving preference (like Subkī) to the version "between spirit and body," also preferred by Sakhāwī.

[55] *Ibid*, I, pp. 72-74, 79-80, VII, p. 245, VIII, pp. 346ff. SUYŪTĪ, 1959, II, pp. 189-190 also notes Subkī's text in a shortened version.

[56] The work in question is *k. al-Nafkh wa l-taswiya*, also known under the title *al-Madnūn al-saghīr*. Other than Ibn Arabī's challenge (1906, I, p. 125) to the work, which categorically asserts that Ghazālī is not the author of the text, a number of doctrinal points addressed in the treatise cast serious doubt on Ghazālī's authorship (cf. WATT, 1952, pp. 36-37).

[57] ZURQĀNĪ, 1996, I, p. 74.

[58] Ibn Taymiyya is here relying on the fact that, according to the versions cited by Ibn Hanbal, the question asked of the Prophet was not *kunta*, but rather *matā kutibta nabiyyan*. On the subject of this hadith's many versions, cf. QASTALLĀNĪ, 1996, I, pp. 63ff, and Zurqānī's commentary that accompanies it.

[59] IBN TAYMIYYA, n.d., II, 4th part, p. 8; the expression "*taqdīru Llāh al-sābiq li-khalqihi*" is a reference to the "writing down of decrees" (*kitābat al-maqādīr*), which is at issue in the famous hadith where the angels write down the destiny of created beings (cf. also Ibn Taymiyya's *Haqīqatu madhhab al-ittihādiyyīn*, pp. 126-127, cited by O. Yahia in an appendix for TIRMIDHĪ, 1965, p. 509).

[60] IBN TAYMIYYA, n.d., II, 4th part, p. 8.

[61] Cf. his "Lettre ouverte au Prophète" transcribed by Nabhānī in AUBKĪ, 1996, pp. 132-133, and the many passages in *Shifā' al-siqām...*, where he challenges Ibn Taymiyya regarding the issue of visiting Prophet's tomb (*ibid.*, pp. 59, 68, 103-104, 132-135).

[62] It is however this very word, *haqīqa*, that Ibn Arabī uses most frequently in reference to the "spiritual entity" of Muhammad. Subkī's teachings were clearly influenced by the Andalusian master, as we shall see.

[63] Cf. IBN AL-KHATĪB, 1970, I, p. 158.

Chapter Two

"In truth, you are of a sublime nature" [1]

"A LIGHT HAS COME TO YOU FROM GOD" [2]

The expression itself – "Muhammadan Light" (*nūr muhammadī*) – has its origin in scriptural references where the correlation is made between the person that the Prophet was and the symbolism of light. In the Qur'an, for example, Muhammad is called a "Resplendent Torch" [3], and several traditions mention luminous phenomena at the time of his conception and birth [4].

As it was, the Doctors of the Law barely fussed over the issue, if at all. Things were very different when it came to the *concept* of "Muhammadan Light," which, in the minds of Muslim spiritual seekers, comes from a meta-historical vision of the Prophet's *risāla* (his "mission"). This view conferred upon Muhammad the *status of primordiality* in the hierarchy of God's Creation, on the one hand, and on the other the role of progenitor, by virtue of which he is the spiritual father of the human race, just as Adam was its physical father. This particular teaching was all the more suspect due to its quite early appearance (in a variety of different wordings) among the Shi'ite "extremists" known as *ghulāt*, especially the Khattābiyya [5].

In any case, my interest here is more concerned with the thoughts of Sunni spiritual thinkers on the concept. Let us take for example the way the author of the *Mawāhib* sums up this teaching so basic to Sufism – a theme whose impact on every area of the Muslim world has been shown by Annemarie Schimmel [6]. Qastallānī is certainly a later writer, but what is interesting about him is that – although he had Sufi connections and helped spread some of their main teachings – he was highly respected by Sakhāwī. The latter – an adversary of Ibn Arabī's if there ever was one, as well as of his followers – was Qastallānī's teacher and praised his student in the *Daw'* [7]. Qastallānī was actually wise enough not to mention Ibn Arabī by name, even when he was borrowing both his vocabulary and his ideas, as is evident:

> He [God], out of the perennial lights in the Abode of Unity, brought the "Muhammadan Reality" (*al-haqīqa al-muhammadiyya*) into being, and then from this Reality He made all the worlds, both the higher and the lower, each according to the form of its status. [...] He then informed him that he was a prophet, and told him of his apostolic mission. This took place while Adam – according to what he [the Prophet] has stated – "was between spirit and body." The essences of all spirits sprang from him. [...] He is thus the genus of all genuses, the supreme father of all "beings" (*mawjūdāt*) and of men. [8]

For readers familiar with his writings, these lines may well call Ibn Arabī to mind, and for good reason. In large part, this passage is little more than a patchwork of lines from '*Anqā*' *mughrib* [9], a treatise Ibn Arabī composed prior to his departure from the Middle East. A number of others have addressed the same subject, but this borrowing from the Shaykh al-Akbar is enlightening in more ways than one. For one, it shines a light on the role that certain popular literature – particularly, that dealing with the figure of the Prophet – played in spreading Ibn Arabī's teachings among the masses, even in the most remote areas of the Muslim world [10]. It also confirms, if confirmation is needed, the particular role that his works played in the history of Sufi teachings, where their prominence is unsurpassed.

We do not know if it was Qastallānī himself who compiled this list of quotes, or if he simply copied it from one of the several collections of excerpts from Ibn Arabī's writings that were most often compiled by anonymous admirers of the *Futūhāt*'s author. Either theory is plausible. What is true is that Ibn Arabī's work was quickly accepted as the reference par excellence for anything related to Islamic hagiology, prophetology, or metaphysics. The first chapter of the *Mawāhib* deals with the "Muhammadan Reality," and it was not just by chance that the chapter opens with a long quote from Ibn Arabī, even if his name was left unmentioned.

Research today is not yet able to state with certainty at what point the theme of *nūr muhammadī*, "Muhammadan Light," appeared. Echoes of it are heard as early as Islam's second century, in a *tafsīr* (Qur'anic commentary) by Muqātil (d. 150/767), which states: "The light that is said to be like 'a niche wherein sits a lamp in a glass [11]' refers to the light of the Prophet as he was still in his father's loins [12]." This is likewise the case for the *tafsīr* text ascribed to Imam Ja'far al-Sādiq (d. 148/765), such as it was recorded by Sulamī (d. 412/1021) [13]. We are indebted to Paul Nwyia, even more than to Massignon, for measuring the "decisive influence" that Ja'far's *tafsīr* had on the birth of the Sufi hermetic tradition. Nwyia not only published the Sunni version of this exegetic corpus [14], but – in later research [15] – he also identified the major principles supporting Ja'far's interpretation of Revelation. On top of all this, it was Nwyia who made note of the imam's commentary on the letter *nūn* – which opens Sura 68 – where the uniqueness of the Prophet's ontological status is connected to the concept of pre-eternal "Muhammadan Light":

> *Nūn* is the pre-eternal Light from which God drew all creatures, and which He conferred to Muhammad. To him it was said "you are of a sublime nature [16]," that is: you were made from light that was attributed to you before eternity [17].

It was Dhū l'Nūn al-Misrī (d. 246/860), according to Massignon's research [18], who undertook the job of editing Ja'far's *tafsīr*. His disciple Sahl al-Tustarī (d. 283/896) apparently knew of the work. In fact, as G. Böwering has remarked, the way he went about the process of textual interpretation was clearly inspired by Ja'far, though for some reason the latter's name was never mentioned [19].

In any case, in regard to Sunni spiritual seekers, it is to Tustarī that we are indebted for the first outline of how the theme of *nūr muhammadī* might have played out. The only first hand document we can rely on currently regarding this issue is his Qur'anic commentary [20], although it is more than probable that he also addressed the theme in his "Book of the Pact" (*Kitāb al-mīthāq*). The latter title was mentioned by one of Ibn Arabī's closest disciples, Ibn Sawdakīn [21], who clarified that the book's subject was the Primordial Pact made between God and men before the beginning of time, in accordance with the famous verse 172 of Sura al-'Araf: "And when your Lord drew their descendants (*dhurriyya*) from the loins of Adam's sons and made them bear witness against themselves: 'Am I not your Lord?,' they replied: 'Certainly, yes.'"

It was actually in reference to this event, which preceded the human race's advent into History [22], that Tustarī described the divine drama that would give birth to Creation – at the center of which the "Light of Muhammad" plays a primordial role. According to him, the word *dhurriyya* (descendants, progeny) here has three meanings:

> A first, a second, and a third. The first is Muhammad, upon whom be Mercy and Peace, for when God decided to create Muhammad, He produced a light from His light, which when it reached the veil of Majesty (*hijāb al-ʿazama*), prostrated itself once before God. From this prostration, He created an immense column of transparent light, like a crystal, as bright on the inside as on the out, within which was the essence of Muhammad. He then remained in service before the Lord of the Worlds for a million years [...]. Thus, He granted him the privilege of contemplating Him for a million years before the beginning of Creation [...] The second is Adam, *whom He created from the light of Muhammad* while He created Muhammad's body from Adam's clay. The third is Adam's progeny [23].

Clearly outlined here are the two main ideas that structure *nūr muhammadī* as a teaching: the idea of the Prophet's primogeniture, on the one hand, and on the other, everything related to his "agentic," or causal role in the birth of the human community. Other than this text, and the much more concise text concerning the first verses of the Sura *al-Najm* – where Tustarī once again mentions the primordial manifestation of the Prophet in the form of a "column of light" [24] (*ʿamūd al-nūr*) – we also have ʿAyn al-Qudāt al-Hamādhānī (d. 525/1131), who says (albeit without offering his source) that Khadir, the immortal errant saint [25], passed the following tradition to both Tustarī and Shaybān al-Raʿī:

> God created Muhammad's light out of His own light. He moulded it perfectly and placed it before Him. This light then sat before God for a thousand years. Every day and every night He cast His eyes upon it seventy thousand times, each time layering it with a new light and a new mercy. From this light He then created all creatures [26].

The mention of Shaybān al-Raʿī is interesting in this context, to say the least, in the sense that his life largely preceded Tustarī's. Though little biographical information is available, at least we know that Shaybān al-Rāʿī was in contact with Sufyān al-Thawrī (d. 161/778) [27]. It might be noted in this regard that, according to

Kamāl Jaʿfar (who unfortunately offers no supporting reference), it was al-Thawrī who coined the expression "column of light" in reference to the Prophet's primogeniture [28].

All this provides evidence of the numerous areas, some blurring into others, out of which the concept of *nūr muhammadī* was emerging. In a more general sense, this was also true of everything related to early Sufi teachings. Though certain works, especially those by Massignon and Paul Nwyia, have highlighted the most prominent aspects of this mysticism just coming into being in the Islamic world, we are far from reaching a deep understanding of its intellectual landscape. Doing so would entail mapping how and where ideas spread and were circulated in the Islamic world during its first three centuries, at a time when several currents of thought were intermingling and individuals from all kinds of milieux interacting. And all this at a time when knowledge spread primarily via word of mouth.

The problem is all the more complicated because both Sunnis and Shiʼites claimed lineage from Imam Jaʿfar, whose teachings deeply influenced the most spiritually inclined members of both communities. Massignon noted that certain "chains of transmission" attribute circulation of one hadith *qudsī* (a hadith directly quoting God) that describes the Prophet's primogeniture as coming from a "handful" (*qabda*) of "Primordial Dust" to which God gave the commandment "Be Muhammad!" (*kūnī Muhammad*) [29]. The idea here is that the Prophet was himself the prime matter or – as the Sufis would say – the "Primordial Dust" (*al-habāʼ*) from which all Creation emerged.

Ibn Arabī says in this regard, in chapter 6 of the *Futūhāt* (where the subject is the "Beginning of the World") that Sahl al-Tustarī and ʿAlī b. Abī Tālib mentioned this "Primordial Dust" [30]. Tustarī deals with the subject in a short work he dedicated to the symbolic qualities of letters [31], which ended up having a lasting influence on later writings about "the science of letters" [32].

"WERE IT NOT FOR YOU, I WOULD NOT HAVE CREATED THE WORLD"

There is not the least doubt that Tustarī's contribution to the practice of reflection on *nūr muhammadī* was significant in Sufism. The concept was described in somewhat obscure terms by Jaʿfar, but present in Islam from very early on. What happened after his time?

Let us note first and foremost that the key idea – that of the Prophet's ontological preeminence – was woven, albeit sometimes in filigree, into the works of spiritual writers even after Jaʿfar's time. Each put his own spin on the motif of the Prophet as an archetype, though prior to Ibn Arabī none attempted to address all the doctrinal implications related to hagiology, prophetology, or eschatology.

Hallāj (d. 309/922), for example, who for a while was a companion of Tustarī's, penned a beautiful passage in praise of the "Muhammadan Luminescence" [33]. In his opinion, there was no doubt about the Prophet being the point of departure for the beginning of creation. Hallāj nevertheless failed to address all the doctrinal consequences of the Prophet's primacy relative to his cosmic role.

Ibn ʿAtāʾ (d. 309/922), who was both a contemporary of Hallāj and a friend, was clearly aware of "Muhammadan Light" as a concept, as he alludes briefly to it in his *tafsīr*. Sulamī mentions this in his remarks about the first verse of Sura 68 – that is, the letter *nūn* that Imam Jaʿfar equates with the pre-eternal "Muhammadan Light" – a passage whose origin he attributes to Ibn ʿAtāʾ. The passage is reminiscent of the imam's interpretation, though worded differently:

> By this he meant: the light of Pre-Eternity out of which He created all lights, and with which He illumined the innermost being [*sirr*] of His beloved [the Prophet], upon him be Mercy and Peace, and the hearts of the *awliyāʾ* of his Community [34].

It is worth mentioning that what we see emerging here is the idea that the saints received some of the grace accorded to the Prophet at the dawn of Creation. There is no doubt that the two exegeses are related. The same observation might be made regarding other passages in Ibn ʿAtāʾ's Qurʾanic Commentary, where Paul Nwyia has pointed out how indebted he was to the individual known as Jaʿfar, and whose writings Ibn ʿAtāʾ had apparently read [35].

Tirmidhī (d. ca. 300/910), on the other hand, did not use the term *nūr muhammadī* [36]. He did however support the idea of the Prophet's ontological primordiality, referring to it as the first thing known, wanted, and mentioned by God [37]. Geneviève Gobillot nevertheless stresses that in Tirmidhī's view, the reason why the Prophet can be seen as the originating principle behind the cosmogonic process is essentially because Muhammad is the *cause* of the universe's coming into existence. The author of "Seal of the Saints" (*Khatm al-awliyā'*) mentions the "joy" that God felt in this regard, the source of which was the Prophet, and which led Him to create Adam [38]. The idea at issue here is thus that the Prophet is the *sabab al-wujūd*, the "Cause of existentiation." The roots of *sabab al-wujūd* were sunk early in Islam, as the concept can be seen in the words of a hadith *qudsī* noted by Tabarānī (d. 360/971) and Bayhaqī (d. 458/1077). Several versions of the hadith exist, one of which goes back to the second caliph, ʿUmar Ibn al-Khaṭṭāb [39]. According to the hadith, after Adam sinned, he begged God's pardon invoking Muhammad's name, which he saw inscribed into the foot of the Throne [40]. In the ensuing dialogue God states: "Were it not for him [Muhammad], I would not have created you." According to another version, one traced back to Salmān al-Fārisī and specifically noted by Ibn ʿAsākir (571/1176), the words were spoken directly to the Prophet; God said: "Were it not for you, I would not have created this lower world" [41]. Subkī, by the way, and later Ibn Hajar al-Haytamī (d. 974/1576), base their claim that it is lawful to ask for the Prophet's intercession "before his creation" (in the physical world) on the former version of this hadith [42].

Ibn Masarra (d. 319/931) favors the idea of *materia prima* – the Arabic *al-habā'*, or "Primordial Dust" – to refer to the pre-existence of the Prophet and his role in bringing the cosmos into existence. This approach is thus more philosophical (in the sense of *hikma* rather than *falsafa*) than is that of Tustarī in his "Treatise on Letters" [43].

Kalābādhī (d. 385/995) does not address this issue in his *Kitāb al-taʿarruf*, nor does Qushayrī (d. 465/1072) in his famous *Risāla*. A reading of Qushayrī's *tafsīr* is similarly fruitless. This of course does not mean that he disagreed with the idea of the Prophet's ontological primordiality.

It is significant that imam Ghazālī's (d. 501/1111) "Tabernacle of Lights" (*Mishkāt al-anwār*) contains not the slightest allusion to the concept of "Muhammadan Light." The work's central theme is nevertheless the "Verse on Light" [44] that so nourished the meditations of Muslim seekers in regard to the *nūr muhammadī*. The evidence suggests that the *Ihyā'*'s author was wary of the theory of the Prophet's pre-existence; he undoubtedly detected a whiff of *batiniyya*, an ideology, let us remember, that gave him the holy creeps.

His brother, Ahmad Ghazālī (d. 520/1126) – one of the great figures of the Sufi tradition in Iran – appeared to have a very different opinion on the matter, based on what we read in the *Tamhīdāt* by ʿAyn al-Qudāt, whom Massignon referred to as his "favorite follower." The *nūr muhammadī* theme is ubiquitous in the work, which ʿAyn al-Qudāt completed just four years before being charged with heresy – and executed, like Hallāj, at the age of thirty-three. He never even tried to elaborate on the topic, as a matter of fact, which seemed to him to be such an established belief. What is additionally remarkable is that ʿAyn al-Qudāt based his opinion essentially on a hadith unknown by the canonical collections, and cited it five times. I have been able to find no trace of the hadith in the writings of Sunni authors discussed above who preceded him, even though he refers explicitly to the idea of *nūr muhammadī*. According to the hadith, one of the Companions, Jābir b. ʿAbd Allāh, had asked the Prophet what the first thing God created was. The Prophet replied: "Oh Jābir, the first thing God created was the light of your Prophet" [46].

There is little need to highlight the correlation between this hadith, whose circulation in Sunni circles appears to have been relatively late, and certain Imamite traditions, like those compiled by Ibn Bābūya (d. 381/991), according to which the Prophet and ʿAlī were created from the same light long before the world became a world [47]; and all the more so since Jābir b. ʿAbd Allāh was held in similarly high esteem among Shi'ite Muslims [48].

The hadith in question would nevertheless end up being widespread in *tasawwuf* literature, at least in the Middle East between the 6th and 12th centuries, to such an extent that it would become, like the *kuntu nabiyyan* hadith, an important scriptural reference about the pre-existence of the Prophet. It shows up a few decades after ʿAyn al-Qudāt, cited by ʿAmmār al-Bidlīsī (d. ca. 600/1200) [49], one of Najm al-Dīn Kubrā's (d. 618/1221) teachers. The latter, in turn, cited it a number of times in the *tafsīr* attributed to him [50]. Najm al-Dīn Rāzī, Kubrā's chosen disciple, used the tradition as support [51] in developing his own dramatic version of *nūr muhammadī*, the final act of which gives rise to the dawn of humanity [52].

Born in Murcia like Ibn Arabī, Ibn Sabʿīn (b. ca. 668/1270) – whose teachings were strongly influenced by the Shaykh al-Akbar, though he never mentioned the fact – offered his own personal interpretation of the "Muhammadan Light" theme. In a short work on "the lights of the Prophet" [53], he attributes a series of thirty-three different lights to the Prophet, each of which is scripturally based on one of Muhammad's privileges: the fact that his name is associated with the Divine Name in the *shahāda*, his "Night Journey," God calling him a "mercy for the worlds [54]," and so forth. These different lights are thus like beams diffracted from a single source – that light belonging rightfully to the "Resplendent Torch."

A contemporary of Kubrā, Ibn Arabī – and we should say this from the start – never mentions the famous hadith that is traced back to Jābir b. ʿAbd Allāh, at least in its most widely known form [55]. The *Futūhāt* author actually sticks to the version from the canonical collections: "The first thing that God created was the Pen (*qalam*)," or, according to another version, "the Intellect" (*al-ʿaql*) [56]. Such is also the case for the Andalusian Sufi Ibn Qasī (d. 546/1151), who at several points in his famous *Khalʿ al-naʿlayn* addresses the question of the Prophet's ontological primordiality. According to Doctor Amrānī (to whose excellent critical edition of the text we are indebted), Ibn Arabī's teaching on *haqīqa muhammadiyya* is greatly dependent on Ibn Qasī's [57].

It is true that the expressions Ibn Qasī uses to refer to the archetypal figure of the Prophet – like "Spirit" (*rūh*) or, less often, "Reality" (*haqīqa*) – appear in the Shaykh al-Akbar's writings. To my knowledge, however, Ibn Arabī does not use the term *nūr muhammadī*. For all that, however, we cannot ignore the frequent, often severe, criticism Ibn Arabī unleashed in regard to his elder in his commentary on Ibn Qasī's *Khalʿ* that he wrote late in life [58]. On the other hand, and this point is essential, nowhere in Ibn Qasī do we find a well-developed doctrine regarding the attributes of the "Muhammadan Reality" and their place in sacred history; this theme does nevertheless play a key role in Ibn Arabī's texts addressing the subject.

In truth, the same observation might be made regarding Ibn Arabī's predecessors as a whole. As this brief overview has suggested, they rarely broach the topic of *nūr muhammadī* other than in the context of the birth of the cosmos; it is as if, once Creation was completed, the archetypal Muhammadan entity – whether it was called "Light," "Spirit," or "Reality" – ceased to be operational.

Notes
_____

[1] Qurʾan, 68:4.

[2] Qurʾan 5:15.

[3] Qurʾan 33:46.

[4] On this subject, see RUBIN's well documented study (1975, pp. 62-119); cf. also CHODKIEWICZ, 1986, ch. 4; ZURQĀNĪ, 1996, I, pp. 190-224.

[5] Cf. MASSIGNON, 1969, I, pp. 568, 584; GOBILLOT, 2000, p. 98.

[6] Cf. SCHIMMEL, 1984, ch. 5.

[7] Cf. IBN AL-ʿIMĀD, 1979, VIII, p. 121.

[8] QASTALLĀNĪ, 1996, I, pp. 52-55.

[9] The sentences are from IBN ARABĪ, 1954, pp. 36,40, 41. As always, Ibn Arabī cites the hadith using its other wording, "between water and clay."

[10] Cf. CHODKIEWICZ, 1994 (a), where a long introduction is devoted to the ways Ibn Arabī's teachings spread.

[11] Qurʾan, 24:35.

[12] Cf. NWYIA, 1991, p. 95. The famous "light verse" gave rise, quite early on, to a number of interpretations where the *nūr muhammadī* appeared. Cf. TABARĪ, n.d., IX, 18th part, pp. 104-111, which cites a relevant tradition traced back to Ibn ʿAbbās; and *ibid.*, IV, 6th part, p. 104, where on the subject of verse 5:15 ("A light has come to you...") Tabarī notes that the light here refers to the Prophet. Cf. also SULAMĪ, 2001, II, p. 45, and NWYIA, 1991, pp. 147, 183, regarding Imam Jaʿfar's interpretation.

[13] On the problem of Shiʿite and Sunni recensions of this *tafsīr*, cf. MASSIGNON, 1968, pp. 201-206; NWYIA, 1991, pp. 156ff.

[14] ID., 1968, pp. 181-230.

[15] ID., 1991, pp. 156-207.

[16] Qurʾan 68:4.

[17] NWYIA, 1991, p. 167; SULAMĪ, 2001, II, p. 343.

[18] MASSIGNON, 1968, pp. 201-206.

[19] BÖWERING, 1980, pp. 141-142.

[20] TUSTARĪ, 2002.

[21] Cf. ABDEL-KADER, 1962, introduction, p. xvii, and the transcription of the Arabic text, p. 40; cf. also JUNAYD, 1983, p. 155.

[22] On this aspect of *mīthāq*, cf. GOBILLOT, 2000, pp. 46ff; for the Imāmite interpretation, cf. AMIR-MOEZZI, 1994, pp. 33ff.

[23] TUSTARĪ, 2002, pp. 68-69; BÖWERING, 1980, pp. 149-151; cf. also DAYLAMĪ, 1962, pp. 33-34, where the text of Tustarī's citation differs somewhat (italics mine).

[24] TUSTARĪ, 2002, p. 156.

[25] Cf, *EI2*, "Khadir."

[26] ʿAYN AL-QUDĀT, 1992, p. 240; note that ʿAyn al-Qudāt claims in this work that he himself had received a hadith directly from Khadir (*ibid.*, p. 275).

[27] Cf. IBN AL-JAWZĪ, 1986, IV, p. 376, num. 911; MUNĀWĪ, 1999, I, pp. 325-327; ABŪ NUʿAYM, 1967, VIII, p. 317. Another anecdote concerning Shaybān al-Rāʿī (reported in IBN AL-JAWZĪ, 1986, IV, p. 376) places him in the presence of the caliph Hārūn al-Rashīd, who was in power from 170/786 until 193/809; IBN ARABĪ, 1911, I, p. 594, moreover reports an interview between Shaybān and imams Shāfiʿī (d. 204/820) and Ibn Hanbāl (d. 241/855).

[28] KAMĀL JAʿFAR, 1974, p. 313. MASSIGNON, 1975, III, p. 301, also suggests this idea, though neither author offers a source for what it is based on.

[29] Cf. MASSIGNON, 1968, p. 237. It may be noted that – in contrast to Ibn Arabī, who cites none of the traditions supporting the *nūr muhammadī* theme – emir

'Abd al-Qādir refers to this *khabar* ('ABD AL-QĀDIR AL-JAZĀ'IRĪ, 1966, II, p. 631). Let us remember that some *ghulāt* identified Fātima as this *kūnī* (MASSIGNON, 1969, I, pp. 568, 584). On this subject, GOBILLOT, 2000, p. 98 cites a passage from *Umm al-kitāb*, a proto-Ismaili treatise dating from Islam's second century. Note also that the idea of *qabda* returned and was much more broadly developed – from a Sunni perspective – in IBN 'AJIBA (d. 1224/1809), 1998, pp. 32, 34, 35.

[30] IBN ARABĪ, 1911, I, p. 119. The words attributed to 'Alī regarding this are cited in SUYŪTĪ, n.d., V, p. 66.

[31] *Risālat al-hurūf*, in KAMĀL JA'FAR, 1974, pp. 366f.

[32] GRIL, 1989, pp. 423ff.

[33] MASSIGNON, 1975, III, pp. 300-305; ERNST, 2010, pp. 124-126.

[34] SULAMĪ, 1986, p. 205. This passage does not appear in Ibn 'Atā''s *tafsīr* edited by P. Nwyia, which relies solely on manuscripts of the *Haqā'iq* for support.

[35] NWYIA, 1986, pp. 25-28.

[36] GOBILLOT, 2002 (b), p. 28.

[37] TIRMIDHĪ, 1992 (b), p. 39; cf. also RADTKE and O'KANE, 1996, p. 102.

[38] GOBILLOT, 2002 (b), p. 28.

[39] RUBIN, 1975, pp. 95, 105-106.

[40] Tirmidhī make a reference to this point in the text cited by GOBILLOT, 2002 (b).

[41] ZURQĀNĪ, 1996, I, pp. 118-120 on this hadith, cf. 'AJLŪNĪ, 1351 A.H., num 2123. IBN AL-JAWZĪ, 1988, p. 27, also cites a variant of this hadith traced back to Ibn 'Abbās. 'AYN AL-QUDĀT, 1992, pp. 75, 238, cites the tradition numerous times. On how widely this version of the hadith had spread among Iranian mystics, cf. ISFARĀYINĪ, 1986, p. 202, note 59. As will be seen later, Ibn Arabī unreservedly sticks to the doctrine expressed in this tradition, though he is reluctant (IBN ARABĪ, 1911, I, p. 137) to confer authentic hadith status to it.

[42] NABHĀNĪ, 1996 (b), pp. 102, 105.

[43] *K. Khawāss al-hurūf*, in KAMĀL JA'FAR, 1978, pp. 311-344 (comments about Tustarī are on pp. 317, 335, 339). Cf. also GRIL, 1989, pp. 423-428. Attribution of this treatise to Tustarī was recently questioned (cf. EBSTEIN & SVIRI, 2011).

[44] Ghazālī nevertheless refers to the Qur'an calling the Prophet a "Resplendent Torch" (GHAZĀLĪ, 1964, p. 51).

[45] 'AYN AL-QUDĀT AL-HAMĀDHĀNĪ, 1992, pp. 130, 169, 229, 238, 226.

[46] On this hadith, quite probably of Shi'ite origin, cf. RUBIN, 1975, pp. 98-104; 'AJLŪNĪ, 1351 A.H., num. 827; and QASTALLĀNĪ, 1996, I, pp. 89ff, who reports another hadith on the same theme, going back to 'Alī; in it, the Prophet is to have said: "I was a light before my Lord fourteen thousand years prior to His creation of Adam."

[47] AMIR-MOEZZI, 1994, pp. 29ff; CORBIN, 1991, I, pp. 98-101; BAR-ASHER, 1999, pp. 130-137.

[48] *EI2*, "Jābir b. 'Abd Allāh"; AMIR-MOEZZI, 1994, pp. 25, 74-75.

[49] Cf. BIDLĪSĪ, 1999 (a), p. 129, and 1999 (b), p. 33. Let us remember that Bidlīsī's teacher was Abū Najīb Suhrawardī (d. 563/1168), who himself was one of Ahmad Ghazālī's followers.

[50] On this subject, cf. BALLANFAT, 2002, pp. 198-201.
[51] A tradition that he cites on the authority of Hasan b. ʿAlī, and not of Jābir b. ʿAbd Allāh (RĀZĪ, N. al-D. al-, 1982, p. 60).
[52] *Ibid.*, p. 61.
[53] IBN SABĪN, 1965, pp. 201-211.
[54] Qurʾan 21:107.
[55] This tradition appears – in full, moreover – in the text of the *Bulghat al-ghawwās* edited by A. Mizyadī (Beirut, 2011, p. 69), but it cannot in any case be attributed to Ibn Arabī, even if he did write a work with the same title (cf. YAHIA, 1964, R.G. 91). Emir ʿAbd al-Qādir cites it a number of times, however (ʿABD AL-QĀDIR AL-JAZĀʾIRĪ, 1966, I, pp. 184, 260, II, pp. 631, 645); in these passages he also cites a tradition found in THAʿLABĪ, n.d., pp. 22-23, addressing the creation of the Prophet out of a "White Pearl" (*durra baydāʾ*) (SCHIMMEL, 1984, p. 127). Ibn Arabī identifies the "White Pearl" as the ʿaql and as the *qalam* (IBN ARABĪ, 1911, I, p. 46, II, p. 130) indicating that he had written a treatise titled "The White Pearl" (ID., 1919, p. 56).
[56] IBN ARABĪ, 1911, II, pp. 95, 395, given that for him the words qalam and ʿaql both stand for the "Muhammadan Reality."
[57] IBN QASĪ, 1997, p. 153.
[58] Ibn Arabī often referred to things Ibn Qasī said with terms like "extreme ignorance" (*jahl mufrit*) and "fallacious statements" (*kalām fāsid*), to name but two (ADDAS, 1989, pp. 77ff).

Chapter Three

"And We have sent you to all of humanity" [1]

"I was a prophet..."

Exceptional for a number of reasons, Ibn Arabī does not stand alone in Islamic mysticism. He was heir par excellence to the Sufi masters who preceded him, and one who reinforced their teachings with unparalleled authority, albeit without necessarily borrowing their language. This is why we find it surprising not to see him address the issue of *nūr muhammadī* using Tustarī's terminology: there is no reference to a "column of light" in his known works, nor does he mention the hadiths so common in other writers on the theme. And yet, the ontological status of the "Muhammadan entity" – and the Prophet's role in the birth of the cosmos – are quite present in the Shaykh al-Akbar's writing. They are nevertheless addressed in two very different manners, affecting both style and vocabulary.

The magnificent prologue to the "Illuminations of Mecca" is a prime example of the first of these, a reflection of the mystic's experience. The author recounts a vision whose episodes are transcribed in rhymed prose, but he does so while drawing on traditional symbolic language and images [2]. The wording the Shaykh al-Akbar uses and the way he writes show a perfect congruence between his point of view and that of his predecessors: the Prophet is referred to as the "very goal and raison d'être for the universe," and it is God Himself who declares: "It is because of you, Muhammad, that I created the universe" [3].

Some of Ibn Arabī's writings, in a more discursive style, were addressed to an audience beyond just his followers. These were for "rational minds" (*ahl al-nazar*), and used a vocabulary more familiar to them, the vocabulary of philosophical speculation that the "Epistles of the Brothers of Purity" had spread throughout Andalusia. Such was the case for chapter 6 of the *Futūhāt* [4]. Without abandoning the traditional lexicon, Ibn Arabī here used language closer to that of the *falsafa*; he equated the "Primordial Dust" with *hayūlā* (from the Greek *hylé*)[5], for example, and at the end of the chapter he makes reference to the Aristotelian categories:

> The beginning of Creation was the "Primordial Dust" [*al-habā'*], within which the first thing to exist was the "Muhammadan Reality" [*al-haqīqa al-muhammadiyya*] proceeding from the Name *al-Rahmān*. Then, through His Light, He manifested Himself to this Dust – which speculative thinkers call the prime matter [*materia prima / al-ʿaql*] – in which the entire universe existed in potentiality. Each thing in this "Dust" received [from this theophany] according to its capacity and its predisposition. And nothing in this "Dust," was closer to Him to receive [the theophany] than was the "Reality" of Muhammad, upon whom be Grace and Peace, which is also called the "Intellect" [*al-ʿaql*]. He is thus the master of the universe and the first to appear in existence [6].

However, from the perspective of his teachings – a perspective entirely oriented toward the question of the spiritual future of humanity – what lies at the crux of the debate regarding teachings of the Prophet's pre-existence is less an attempt to determine the *mode of being* of the "Muhammadan Reality," and its role in begetting the universe, than it is to discern its *reason for being*, that is, the *permanent* role it is called to play.

It is specifically to this transhistoric magisterium, one which transcends historical bounds, that the enigmatic *kuntu nabiyyan* ("I was a prophet") refers, according to Ibn Arabī. He reminds us that God's Messenger did not say "I was a man [*insān*]" or "I was a being [*mawjūd*]"; he declared "I was a *prophet* [*nabī*]." Given that we are dealing with a hadith here, there is no chance that one word, rather than another, happened to be used just randomly: God's Messenger is, absolutely, a "pure servant" (*ʿabd mahd*). Consequently, since he is devoid of any will of his own and of any individuality, the Prophet – when he addresses his Community – is never anything other than God's spokesperson, the carrier of His word. The "Sayings" of God's Messenger are invested with the same divine revelation status as are Qur'anic verses [7]. Whence the importance that Ibn Arabī gives to the word-for-word transmission of the utterance (*matn*) of a hadith [8]: when it comes to divine discourse, even the slightest, most elementary particle has meaning.

In other words, the form of the utterance takes on a primordial importance in Ibn Arabī's hermeneutic process. He does not look for anything "*beyond the letter elsewhere than within the letter itself* [9]." Hence, regarding the question – of serious consequence, as we shall see – about knowing what *kuntu nabiyyan* actually means, he goes about finding the answer in the obvious way. The *Futūhāt* texts that touch on this issue are myriad. Here are a few examples:

> He said "I was a prophet." He did not say "I was a man," or "I was a being." [...] He thus made clear that prophecy [*nubuwwa*] resided within him before the creation of those prophets who are *substitutes* [*nuwwāb*] in this lower world [10].

> What he meant was that he knew this because God had him know his rank [*martaba*] while he was still a spirit, while bodies had not yet been created. Just as He made the Alliance with Adam's sons before creating their bodies [...]. *In the same way the prophets who were in the world are his substitutes, from Adam up to the last among them* [11].

> In regard to the spiritual station [*maqām*] [of prophecy], Adam and all those coming after him are no more than Muhammad's *heirs*, for Muhammad was a prophet while Adam – who was still between water and clay – did not yet exist. Prophecy [*nubuwwa*] thus belonged to Muhammad at a time when there was no Adam, just as the Adamic human form belonged to Adam at a time when the Prophet did not yet have a corporal form. Adam is thus the father of human bodies and Muhammad is the father of [spiritual] heritage; such will be the case from the time of Adam until that moment when this heritage comes to an end. And therefore all Divine Law that has appeared and all knowledge [of a spiritual order] are the products of the Prophet's heritage [*mīrāth muhammadī*], *in all ages and from all messengers and prophets until the Day of Resurrection* [12].

> He said: "I was a prophet while Adam was still between water and clay," while everyone other than him became a prophet only upon the bestowal of his prophetic authority and at the time of his apostolic mission [13].

In other words, *kuntu nabiyyan* is not simply a reference to the fact that the Prophet had a form of existence before he was present in a way that could be perceived by the senses; the word *nabī* would have been superfluous if such were the case. In fact, this is the case for all human beings who, Ibn Arabī reminds us, pledged their allegiance to God – which assumes a mode of being – at a time when they did not yet have a physical existence.

What this hadith means, literally, is that *nubuwwa* was granted to Muhammad even before the first man was created *ad extra – that nubuwwa thus belongs to him alone, fully and completely*. Being a *nabī* [prophet] includes being a *walī* [saint], in the sense that any prophet is eminently "close to God" [14]. Accession to *nubuwwa* consequently implies both *the exercise of spiritual authority* and *the attainment of some degree of spiritual perfection*. In the case of the former, given the primordial nature of the divine investiture bestowed upon the Prophet, we are dealing with the highest spiritual magisterium; in the case of the latter, similarly – and surpassing all others – at issue is the highest degree of sanctity.

What follows from this, on the one hand, is that all those who at some point in history assume duties of a spiritual nature – most notably, God's "messengers" in the broad sense of the term – are invested with this role as "substitutes" of the *rūh muhammadī*; what follows on the other hand is that everything men are given to know and experience on the spiritual plane – regarding knowledge, states, charismata, and so forth – comes from his "spiritual heritage."

Whence the two key ideas underlying Ibn Arabī's argument in the passages cited. The author of *Seal of the Saints* explained the decisive role these ideas played in his hagiological and prophetological teachings: one was the concept of *niyāba*, "substitution" connected to the first aspect of this transhistorical magisterium; and the other had to do with the concept of *wirātha*, "spiritual heritage," which relates to the second.

Niyāba, as we have seen, is a concept referring to the idea that all of God's prophets and messengers who preceded Muhammad in this world were "representatives" – at a certain point in History – of the *rūh muhammadī,* the Muhammadan Spirit, to which God granted spiritual sovereignty for all eternity, though it does not exercise this sovereignty fully except in the person of the "Seal of the Prophets," Muhammad. It is in this sense that Muhammad exercised his spiritual authority at all points in the history of the world – subtly, at the beginning, and more openly later:

[The spirit of Muhammad] was thus present in the "world of Mystery" [*ʿālam al-ghayb*] without existing in the "world of Manifestation" [*ʿālam al-shahāda*]. And God informed him of his being a prophet and told him of this while Adam was still, as he has said, "between water and clay." The cycle governed by the status of His name "the Hidden" [*al-bāṭin*] occurred for Muhammad when his body was made one with his spirit, and appeared. Authority was then transmitted to the status of His name "the Apparent" [*al-ẓāhir*], which has been governing the cycle of time since that point. He thus held authority occultly at first, by means of divine laws brought by the prophets, and then openly [...] [15].

In other words, Muhammad is, as Subkī had said, the "Prophet of prophets" (*nabiyyu al-anbiyāʾ*), for the very reason that God chose him above all others, at the beginning of beginnings. This is a spiritual supremacy made evident by, according to the Shafiʿī qadi, the pact made between God and His prophets (*mīthāq al-anbiyāʾ*). Revelation refers to it by saying "And when God made this arrangement with the prophets, He said 'I am giving you a Book, and wisdom; and then *a messenger* (*rasūl*) will come to you, and he will confirm what you have received. Believe in him, and assist him. Do you consent to this pact, and accept its conditions?' They replied 'We do consent.' – 'Then bear witness; I bear witness with you'" [16].

It goes without saying that the lack of grammatical specificity for the word *rasūl* has been fodder for numerous debates among exegetes. Some are of the opinion that here it means "any of God's messengers," and that the verse is consequently saying that the prophets were committing to supporting one another. This is Tabarī's opinion, for example [17]. Other commentators have argued that Revelation has offered numerous examples where the word *rasūl*, while indeterminate, is unquestionably referring to the Prophet, whom they believe is the subject of this pact through which the entire community of prophets solemnly recognized his spiritual sovereignty. This is the reading – supported by traditions attributed to ʿAlī and Ibn ʿAbbās – that both Qurṭubī [18] (d. 671/1272) and Subkī prefer.

But while Qurṭubī limits himself to confirming Muhammad's pre-eminence as established by this "pact," Subkī – who wrote a commentary on this Qurʾanic passage in a little work later reproduced by Nabhānī [19] – uses it as a scriptural foundation for a prophetology with clearly Akbarian tones (though this may not be apparent at first glance). Subkī is in no way a teacher of Sufism; his always somewhat convoluted writing style is that of a jurist. Thus, he begins with extensive comments on this series of verses from the (somewhat reductionist) historical perspective of Muslim scholars. From this point of view, *mīthāq al-anbiyā'* means that, in case Muhammad's prophetic authority should at some point coincide with that of other prophets, they would *de facto* be under his jurisdiction. An actual case of this happening has arisen only once: at the time of the "Night Voyage," when, according to what Tradition tells us [20], God's Messenger led the prayer with the other prophets standing behind him.

Up to this point, Subki's exegesis is both lacking in originality and strictly in line with the ulama's beliefs [21]. After an extensive excursus, the conclusions he reaches thus come quite unexpectedly:

> He [God] made them take an oath so that they would know that he [Muhammad] takes precedence over them *and that he is their prophet and their messenger* [22].

Subkī subsequently compared the contract that the prophets thus entered into regarding Muhammad to the "pledge of allegiance" (*bay'a*) owed to the caliph, and suggested that the former may have been the origin of the latter. Whatever the case, this leads us to believe that Muhammad's *risāla* "embraces all creatures, *from Adam to the Day of Resurrection*; the earlier prophets and their respective communities *thus belong to his umma* and the laws brought by these prophets make up His Law for these communities" [23]. It is true that Subkī's interpretation was considered "singular" (*gharīb*) [24] by his contemporaries, who were far from unanimous in agreeing with it; apparently, they were unaware that Ibn Arabī was the source of the interpretation.

The assertion that all divine laws promulgated – from the beginning of time until the Prophet began his preaching – are specific manifestations of the Prophet's universal Law is a recurrent theme for the author of the *Futūhāt*. This Law did not have its complete, definitive form until Qur'anic revelation began:

> When he appeared, he was like the sun in whose light all other light is lost, and he confirmed what he confirmed of the [earlier] laws that he had instituted via his substitutes, and he abrogated what he abrogated [25].

His Law encompasses all laws, for he was a prophet when Adam had not yet been created. From Him come the laws of all the other prophets, who are his messengers and his substitutes on earth, because of his physical absence. Had he been present in body, no [prophet] would have had a Law outside of his [26].

All the divine laws that they [the prophets] have brought proceed from his Law under His name "the Hidden" [al-bātin], for he was a prophet when "Adam was between water and clay" [27].

"I CAME INTO BEING FOR ALL MEN" [28]

"I was a prophet when Adam was between water and clay" would echo the famous verse from Sura 34, which proclaims "We have sent you to all of humanity" [29]. Understood literally, this verse is actually incompatible with the point of view that the Prophet's intervention during the course of humanity's spiritual history dates from the 6th century of the common era. If his spiritual authority had not been in effect since the beginnings of the human Odyssey, Revelation could not lay claim to the absolute universality of his mission.

There are two possibilities here: either one admits the transhistorical nature of his mission – which, according to Ibn Arabī, the literal meaning of the *kuntu nabiyyan* hadith is referring to, and upon which the idea of *niyāba* is based – in which case it is legitimate to say that he was sent for *the totality of* men; or this idea is rejected, in which case one is forced to exclude all those who lived in times previous to the Prophet's spiritual "jurisdiction." One consequence of this latter case is that one is also forced to overlook the obvious meaning of the verse; this exegetical procedure is preferred by the doctors of the Law: "In this regard, [The ulama] as a whole, says Zurqānī, are of the opinion that 'the totality of men' should be understood as *beginning in their lifetime* and up to the final Day" [30].

Ibn Arabī finds himself unable to accept this distortion of the literal meaning, as it radically diminishes the highly universal extent of the proclamation:

He was sent to *the totality of men*, according to the text [of the Book]. He [God] did not say "We have sent you to this particular community," nor did He say "We have sent you to the men of your time and to all those who will come later, up to the Day of

Resurrection." What He told him was that He had sent him to *the totality of* men. Now "totality of men" goes from Adam up to the last of men [31].

He was sent to *the totality of men*, which was accorded to none other than him, and this includes men since the time of Adam up to the last man [to come] [32].

The Community of Muhammad is not his tribe. His Community is all those to whom he was sent. Now Muhammad was sent to all men. All are thus part of his Community, regardless of the nation they belong to [33].

It is important to note here that the *Futūhāt*'s author is setting up a correlation between the *kuntu nabiyyan* hadith – which, in affirming the principle of the Prophet's ontological preeminence, also lays a foundation for the strongly universal nature of his mission – and the prefatory Sura of the Qur'an, *al-Fātiha* ("That which opens"), which he says sums up and synthesizes all previous revelations and, in so doing, is a vehicle for Truth in the most universal of all possible ways [34].

Far from confining his thoughts to platitudes and banalities, Ibn Arabī's respect for literal meaning led him to articulate one of the boldest ideas in all his teaching, that of the strict universality "in both time and space" [35] of Muhammad's *risāla*. From his point of view, in other words, all of humanity constitutes the *umma*, the "Community of the Prophet."

His position was bold, in the sense that the *Futūhāt*'s author was the first to outline, in terms both clear and precise, a position regarding what he calls *shumūl al-umma*, according to which the human race as a whole belongs to the Community of the Prophet. A number of spiritual thinkers before him probably shared the same view, but none appears to have put it in writing. Rather, we may assume that they observed a certain amount of what might be called "self-imposed restraint" – completely understandable in this case, since believing in a "universal" *umma* would not be without consequence when it came to the (serious) question of the posthumous future of humanity.

Whatever the case, a number of later authors who were masters of *tasawwuf* – and not only those directly connected to the Shaykh al-Akbar's school – quickly adopted the teaching as their own, and with no more hesitation than Ibn Arabī had shown [36] (even if, as we shall soon see, they did not all take the plunge into its eschatological implications). However, it is not their words I will cite in concluding my remarks on this point – as might in fact be expected – but rather the more unexpected words of Subkī, whose intellectual courage goes so far as to admit his past errors:

> Thus, the previously hidden meaning of two hadiths becomes clear. One concerns his words: "I came into being for all men." We had been of the opinion that this meant beginning with his time and up to the Last Day. It appears rather that this [includes] all men, *from the first of them to the last.*

> The second concerns his words: "I was a prophet when Adam was between spirit and body." We were of the opinion that this referred to knowledge [that God had of his prophetic nature], though it appears there is more to it than this [...] [37].

"More to it than this" in this case meant the Prophet's *haqīqa* which, as will be remembered, was "present from that time on, even though his physical presence did not arise until later" [38].

There is no doubt in my mind that Subkī had at least indirect access to Ibn Arabī's teachings. Let us not forget that he was a known adversary of Ibn Taymiyya, and was especially opposed to the latter's disparagement of veneration for the Prophet. The Hanbali polemicist filled hundreds of pages for the sole purpose of countering the Shaykh al-Akbar's heresy...richly supported by quotes, which thus helped to spread the ideas he was attempting to counter. At least in this manner (and perhaps via other channels, though this remains to be shown), Subkī was introduced to the key ideas in Ibn Arabī's teaching on the "Muhammadan Reality." For the most part, Subkī agrees with him. This is true regarding the *kuntu nabiyyan* hadith, where he offers an interpretation that is basically in line with Ibn Arabī's, as it also is in regard to the *niyāba* of the prophets, who he believed were only carrying out their mandate as "substitutes" for Muhammad, which led him to supporting the *actual* universality of the *risāla* of the Prophet.

Does the name of this honorable scholar deserve being added to the list of Ibn Arabī's "partisans"? There would at least appear to be no risk in adding it to what might, at first glance, be the less exclusive list of ulama who quietly contributed to spreading certain key ideas from his teachings, even if on other occasions they might have been calling him a heretic [39].

I should say *some* key ideas, but not all; there is one fundamental aspect of Ibn Arabī's prophetology that shows up nowhere in Subkī's work: that dealing with the idea of *walāya* ("sainthood"), and related idea of *wirātha* ("spiritual heritage"). Without going too deeply into this subject, which has already been studied in depth [40], let us remember a few of Ibn Arabī's essential ideas on these issues.

Anyone familiar with the Shaykh al-Akbar's work would notice that semantics play a major role in his doctrinal thought. This is particularly the case when he discusses the relationship between *walāya* ("sainthood") and *nubuwwa* (prophecy/being a prophet). The *Futūhāt*'s author stressed the fact, on numerous occasions [41], that the word *nubuwwa* – and thus also the word *nabī* – can be seen in two different ways, depending on whether it is used in a limited, or in a broader, sense. In the case of the former, it refers to a role played specifically by prophets who are acting with lawmaking authority. It has this meaning in the famous hadith: "Apostolic mission [*risāla*] and prophecy [*nubuwwa*] have now ceased to exist; no apostle and no prophet will come after me" [42].

In the second case, it has the meaning referred to in the other hadith, where "dreaming" (*ru'ya*) is one of the forty-six parts of *nubuwwa* [43]. From what we can see, the issue here is no longer prophecy in the strict sense – that which involves proclaiming a Divine Law, and thus a role played by no one other than Muhammad – but prophecy in the more general sense, where what is being referred to is a spiritual *station* (*maqām*), the most elevated of all stations, according to Ibn Arabī, and the one representing the highest level of sanctity. *Nubuwwa* in this case is thus a synonym for *walāya*; when we look at it from this perspective, we understand that it remains accessible to believers, although only a small number of them – those whom Ibn Arabī calls the "prophet-saints" – will reach this degree of spiritual realization.

What it is important to remember is that for Ibn Arabī the *kuntu nabiyyan* hadith – upon which he based his *haqīqa muhammadiyya* doctrine, as we have seen – refers to *both* of these aspects of *nubuwwa*. In other words, just as prophecy in the strict sense was conferred upon Muhammad while Adam was "still between water and clay," so also was *walāya*, "sainthood," bestowed upon him at the dawn of Creation [44]. From this perspective, the Prophet – or, to be more precise, the "Muhammadan Spirit" that existed while

THE HOUSE OF THE PROPHET

Adam was still "between water and clay" and of which Muhammad, the person, would be the full and complete manifestation during Historical Time – is the primordial source of holiness from which all the saints who ever were and all those still to come until the Final Day would draw, regardless of the tradition they belong to. Emergent from the flesh of Adam, they are – to different degrees – the spiritual sons of the Prophet and his direct heirs.

"FROM PROPHET TO PROPHET..."

In comparison to the often precise yet always disparate phrasing found in the writings of his predecessors who addressed the pre-existence of the Prophet, Ibn Arabī's many studies devoted to the issue show considerable evolution: what was a certainly primordial and omnipresent idea in the meditations of spiritual writers from Islam's first century – but with descriptions as varied as they were imprecise – became a singularly elaborated doctrine with terminology that was both rich and precise.

The idea of the "Muhammadan Reality" has an essential place in the hierarchy of the Shaykh al-Akbar's hagiological teachings, and likewise, in a more general sense, in his initiatory teachings, by which I mean everything in his writings that pertains to the spiritual journey properly speaking; he sees the "Muhammadan Spirit" as the matrix for all spiritual life. This aspect of the issue was never explained by his predecessors, who saw the pre-existence of the Prophet in respect to his ontological primordiality, on the one hand, and to his contribution in begetting humanity on the other. Rather than reject this point of view (which the *Futūhāt's* author fits into his idea of cosmogenesis) he goes on to address *the primordiality of the Prophet's spiritual status*, by which he explains the universality of Muhammad's *risāla* and, accordingly, that of the *umma*, the "Community of the Prophet."

As they are explained by Ibn Arabī, and with such insistence that their fundamental importance in his eyes leaves no question, these two ideas – those of *shumūl al-risāla* and, following from it, *shumūl al-umma* – appear to be what some have called innovative. The overriding idea of *niyāba*, moreover, had not previously been developed with any depth as a teaching.

The fact nevertheless remains that the main concept of which this idea is the vehicle – that is, that the Muhammadan Spirit "dwelled" within the world since the beginning of time *via* prophets, one following after the other from age to age – had long been around by Ibn Arabī's time, since we see it expressed in a variety of ways as early as Islam's second century.

Parallel to the theme of the primogeniture of the "Muhammad-an entity," another idea – that of its wandering through time – took shape even more broadly. "Carried" from prophet to prophet, this "entity" made its way from Adam to its final dwelling place with its epiphany in the person of Muhammad. Numerous are the hadiths that reference this *verus propheta* theme (it made its appearance quite early in Christianity [45]), and – in contrast to those dealing with the concept of *nūr muhammadī*, which were seen as suspect by the Doctors of the Law and were essentially entrenched in Sufi circles – they were commonly accepted by even the ulama, who frequently cited them.

It is true that their scriptural declarations were questioned less often. Other than Bukhārī, whose *Sahīh* mentions a hadith where the Prophet claimed to have been carried from "generation to generation" (*qarnan faqarnan*) up until the time of his manifestation [46], Ibn Sa'd reports a similar statement attributed to Ibn 'Abbas, who commented: "That is, from prophet to prophet (*min nabiyyin ilā nabiyyin...*), until He makes you manifest as a prophet" [47]. He was referring to verse 219 of Sura *al-Shu'arā'*, where the subject is the "transferral" of the Prophet "among those who prostrate themselves" (*taqallubaka fī l-sājidīn*).

We might also mention Ibn 'Abbas, who was the source of another tradition, this one reported by none other than Ibn al-Jawzī and the qadi 'Iyād [48]: the Prophet had been asked where he was when Adam was in Paradise, and replied "I was in his loins; I was there during the time he was allotted on earth, and I was on the Ark in Noah's loins, and I was thrown into the fire in the loins of Abraham."

Ibn Qutayba attributes to the Prophet's uncle, 'Abbās, a poem about the journey of the prophetic seed deposited in Adam's loins and then carried from generation to generation by a long line of Muhammad's forebears [49].

Other traditions, particularly those reported by Tha'labī (d. 427/1035) [50], maintain that all the Prophet's later ancestors had a light on their foreheads, a manifest sign of Muhammad's presence.

Granted, these sources are not all saying the same thing. Some are referring to the individuals who preceded the Prophet in flesh and blood, and the others to his spiritual genealogy. At issue in some of them is the seminal fluid from which Muhammad would be conceived; in others it is a light emanating from "bearers." All nevertheless express the same idea: that in one way or another the Prophet has been present in the world from the earliest time of the human race; and he will not cease to play his role until the end of this time, according to a widely shared belief that his death – should it mark an end to the physical, momentary manifestation of his presence – will have no bearing whatsoever on his spiritual radiance.

It is in any case remarkable that Ibn Arabī – whose writings teem with citations drawn from hadiths – makes not the slightest allusion to any of these traditions in texts where he addresses the question of niyāba. Niyāba is, when all is said and done, a reformulation in doctrinal terms of the theme of verus propheta. The theme may not have originated in esoteric Islam, of course, but it has richly nourished the teachings of Muslim spiritual writers in matters dealing with the metahistorcal role that they considered the Prophet to play.

Thus, both Tustarī and Ibn ʿAtāʾ were of the opinion that the Prophet was present in Adam's loins when Adam disobeyed God, and it is in this context that both writers are interpreting the second verse of Sura 48 when it says: "So that God may forgive you for your past and future shortcomings." "This means," says Tustarī, "what came before the sin of your father Adam, because you were in his loins, and what followed from the sins of your Community, for you are its guide" [51]. It must be noted that, in the opinion of several commentators, this was the interpretation that ʿAtāʾ al-Khurasānī (d. 135/752), one of the first of Qurʾanic commentators, preferred [52].

This verse from Sura al-Fath ("Victory") has been interpreted in any number of ways, by theologians and Sufis alike. It actually is best categorized as mutashābihāt, referring to verses considered ambiguous because they can be read in ways that seem to contradict points of dogma; the Qurʾan says [53] that God alone knows their true hermeneutic. In this case, the debate centers on the somewhat thorny question of the Prophet's ʿisma, his "impeccability," or more specifically, the extent of his impeccability. If it is generally assumed that the prophets were not susceptible to kabāʾir ("major sins") – at least starting from the moment they are endowed with their prophetic missions – theologians are in disagreement both about whether this impeccability also includes 'minor sins" (*saghā'ir*) during the time of their prophetic mandate, and about the exact definition of what constitutes a minor sin [54]. This helps explain the many debates that interpretation of the verse gave rise to; qadi 'Iyād – who supported the idea of total prophetic impeccability both before and after their missions – devotes a number of pages in his *Shifā'* to discussing them [55].

At the end of the day, most of the ulama are of the opinion that the sins in question were "inadvertent errors" (*sahwan*) committed before the Prophet received Revelation (whence the *mā taqaddama*, "what came before") and afterwards (*mā ta'akhkhara*, "what came after") or, according to a similarly widespread interpretation, before the Hudaybiyya expedition – at the end of which the verse is said to have been revealed – and thereafter [56]. The "clear victory" (*fathan mubīnan*) mentioned in the first verse, which the subordinate conjunction *li* connects to the divine absolution bestowed upon the Prophet ("Indeed We have granted you a clear victory, O Prophet. So that God may forgive you...") is in reference to the conquest of Mecca that would take place three years later [57].

This exegesis takes the "circumstances of Revelation" (*asbāb al-nuzūl*) into account without any implications for the essential parts of 'isma dogma strictly speaking, though it does completely wipe away one aspect of the Qur'anic message that is fundamental to Sufi hermenentics: that of its permanent relevance. Without denying that the Prophet might have inadvertently committed an occasional minor sin [58], the *tasawwuf* masters have tended to say that verses like this [59] are actually cases of God scolding the Prophet's Community [60], through the person of the Prophet.

As we shall see, this is the position Ibn Arabī takes, except that for him, the Prophet's *umma* is humanity in its entirety. In other words, the sins for which the Prophet is blamed in this verse are the ones that men committed both *before* and *after* he walked among them on earth. Consequently, the divine pardon he was granted for his sins is the pardon that, thanks to him, *all men without exception* will receive, even if it comes at the end of time.

Notes

[1] Qur'an 34:28.
[2] Valsan has offered a richly annotated translation of this text (1953, p. 300-311).
[3] IBN ARABĪ, 1911, I, pp. 2, 4.
[4] We are indebted to CHITTICK (1989, pp. 77-93) for a richly annotated translation of this chapter.
[5] Cf. above, p. 32.

[6] IBN ARABĪ, 1911, I, pp. 118-119; the French translation used for the current English translation is primarily based on that of Chodkiewicz, 1986, p. 88.

[7] GRIL, 2005.

[8] IBN ARABĪ, 1911, I, pp. 248, 403.

[9] CHODKIEWICZ, 1994 (a), p. 34.

[10] IBN ARABĪ, 1911, I, pp. 143-144.

[11] *Ibid.*, pp. 134-135 (italics mine).

[12] *Ibid.*, III, pp. 456-457 (italics mine).

[13] *Ibid.*, p. 141.

[14] It should be remembered that the word *walāya*, usually translated by "sanctity" or "sainthood," as well as its root word *walī*, "saint," has the etymological meaning of "proximity" or "closeness"; this issue was discussed at length in CHODKIEWICZ, 1986, ch. I; on the relationship between *nabī* and *walī*, cf. especially pp. 45-46.

[15] IBN ARABĪ, 1911, I, p. 143.

[16] Qur'an, 3:81 (italics mine). The *mīthāq al-anbiyā'* is also alluded to in Qur'an 33:7, the verse where the Prophet's name precedes Noah's and those of the prophets who came after him; in regard to this, Tabarī cites the hadith "I was the first prophet created and the last to be sent" (TABARĪ, n.d., X, 21st part, p. 79). Ibn Arabī remarks that this "pact among the prophets" constitutes the first *mīthāq*, since it took place before Adam's appearance, while the Covenant, by which all men without exception pledged allegiance to God, occurred after he was created, which thus makes it the second *mīthāq* (IBN ARABĪ, 1911, IV, p. 58).

[17] Tabarī cites the many "readings" of this verse (TABARĪ, n.d., III, 3rd part, pp. 236ff); cf. also RĀZĪ, F. al-D., n.d., IV, 8th part, p. 114.

[18] QURTUBĪ, 1933-1950, II, 4th part, pp. 124-125.

[19] Cf. NABHĀNĪ, 1998, I, pp. 509ff.

[20] Cf. *EI2*, "Mi'rāj."

[21] It is best seen in Rāzī and Qurtubī (see above notes 17, 18).

[22] "*Li ya'lamū annahu al-muqaddam 'alayhim wa annahu nabiyyuhum wa rasūluhum*" (NABHĀNĪ, 1998, I, p. 510; QASTALLĀNĪ, 1996, VIII, p. 347; italics mine).

[23] NABHĀNĪ, 1998, I, p. 509; QASTALLĀNĪ, 1996, I, p. 79, VIII, p. 349.

[24] On this subject, cf. annotations in ZURQĀNĪ, 1996, I, p. 79.

[25] IBN ARABĪ, 1911, III, p. 142.

[26] IBN ARABĪ, 1911, II, p. 134.

[27] *Ibid.*, p. 125.

[28] BUKHĀRĪ, "salāt," 56, I, 1st part, p. 95.

[29] Qur'an 34:28. Another verse (7:158) likewise states, "Say: Oh men, I am the Messenger of God for all of you"; similar wording is found in the hadith, for example, "I came into being for all men."

[30] ZURQĀNĪ, 1996, VIII, p. 347.

[31] IBN ARABĪ, 1911, II, p. 139 (italics mine).

[32] *Ibid.*, p. 134 (italics mine).

[33] *Ibid.*, p. 621; cf. also IV, p. 155, III, p. 414, where Ibn Arabī points out that Muhammad's Community encompasses all those who follow "a prophet, a Book,

a single page, any revelation from God."

[34] *Ibid.*, II, p. 134. In ID., 1988, p. 177, Ibn Arabī points out that Sura *al-Fātiha* was granted to Muhammad but not to other prophets, precisely because of the primordial nature of his spiritual magisterium, and that he is consequently *miftāh al-anbiyāʾ*, the "key of prophets."

[35] *Fī l-makān wa l-zamān* is the expression used by shaykh M. Amīn al-Kurdī (d. 1914), who made this teaching about the universality of Muhammad's *risāla* an article of faith (KURDĪ, 1995, p. 68).

[36] For example, HAQQĪ, n.d., VII, p. 294; IBN KĪRĀN, 1999, p. 57; BALLANFAT, 2002, p. 207.

[37] QASTALLĀNĪ, 1996, VIII, p. 350 (italics mine).

[38] See above, pp. 23-24.

[39] In regard to this, cf. above, p. 37, note 10; KNYSH, 1997, pp. 129-130.

[40] Cf. CHODKIEWICZ, 1986; on the concept of *walāya*, cf. especially ch III: on that of *wirātha*, cf. ch. V.

[41] IBN ARABĪ, 1911, II, p. 3, I, p. 545.

[42] WENSINCK, 1936-1969, II, p. 260.

[43] *Ibid.*, p. 338.

[44] This is why IBN ARABĪ (1980, p. 64) asserts that the "Seal of Muhammadan Sainthood" – which in his view is a manifestation of *rūh muhammadī* (CHOD-KIEWICZ, 1986, pp. 155-156) – existed when "Adam was between water and clay"; cf. also the commentary on the *Fusūs* in JANDĪ, 1982, pp. 247-248. Note that Tirmidhī similarly asserts the ontological primordiality of the "Seal of the Saints," and in terms identical to those he used (just a few lines earlier) in talking about that of the "Seal of Messengers" (RADTKE & O'KANE, 1996, p. 102, 110; TIRMIDHĪ, 1965, pp. 39, 45).

[45] CIRILLO, 1981.

[46] BUKHĀRĪ, "*manāqib*," 23, II, 4th part, p. 189.

[47] IBN SAʿD, 1904-1917, I, 1st part, p. 5; another recension, noted by IBN KATHĪR, 1999, V, p. 215, mentions *min sulbi nabiyyin ilā sulbi nabiyyin*, "from the loins of a prophet to the loins of a prophet," thus emphasizing the physical aspect of this transmission. It should in any case be understood that what is at issue here is a physical journey – where the "carriers" were the corporal compartments of the "Muhammadan Entity" – that transferred, according to some traditions, the seminal fluid that would ultimately result in the procreation of the Prophet. Cf. also RUBIN, 1975, pp. 80-81; AMIR-MOEZZI, 1994, p. 169, note 205; QASTALLĀNĪ, 1996, I, pp. 128, 326-330.

[48] IBN AL-JAWZĪ, 1988, p. 27; ʿIYĀD, n.d., 1st part, p. 167; RUBIN, 1975, p. 73.

[49] RUBIN, 1975, p. 90; IBN AL-JAWZĪ, 1988, p. 28; ʿIYĀD, n.d., 1st part, p. 167. The *Matāliʿ al nūr* written by ʿAbdī Efendi (d. 1054/1644) include an interesting summary of the scriptural sources relating to this question and the debates to which the sources gave rise; J. Dreher published an excellent critical edition of the work (ʿABDĪ EFENDĪ AL-BUSNĀWĪ, 2013).

[50] THAʿLABĪ, n.d., pp. 23-34; IBN AL-JAWZĪ, 1988, p. 27; QASTALLĀNĪ, 1996, VII, p. 88. Regarding the theme of the voyage fo the "Muhammadan Light" in the Imamī tradition, cf. AMIR-MOEZZI, 1994, pp. 38-43.

[51] TUSTARĪ, 2002, p. 147. There are different recensions of the commentary these two authorities offer regarding the verse in question. SULAMĪ, 2001, II, p. 254 attributes the following statement to Ibn 'Atā': *mā kāna min dhanbi abīka idh kunta fī sulbihi hīna bāshara al-khatī'a wa mā ta'akhkhara min dhunūb ummatika idh kunta qā'iduhum*"; the same text appears in NWYIA, 1986, p. 146. On the other hand, SULAMĪ, 1986, p. 177, attributes the following statement to Tustarī: "*dhanbu abīka Adām min naslihi fa innahu bika yatawassalu wa mā ta'akhkhara min dhunūb ummatika...*".

[52] For example, QURTUBĪ, 1933-1950, VIII, 16th part, p. 263; HAQQĪ, n.d., IX, p. 8; ZURQĀNĪ, 1996, IX, p. 19. On 'Atā' al-Khurasānī, cf. ZIRKLĪ, 1984, IV, p. 235; IBN AL-'IMĀD, 1979, I, p. 192.

[53] Qur'an 3:7.

[54] On this thorny question, cf. W. Madelung's article in *EI2*, "'*isma*," which reviews the different theories proposed regarding the subject.

[55] Cf. 'IYĀD, n.d., 2nd part, pp. 117-174; cf. also LAMATĪ, 1984, II, pp. 292-293, which includes an anecdote that sheds light on the problems in interpretation this verse poses.

[56] For example, RĀZĪ, F. al-D. al-, n.d., XIV, 28th part, pp. 77-79; QURTUBĪ, 1933-1950, VIII, 16th part, pp. 262-263; TABARĪ, n.d., XI, 26th part, pp. 42ff; HAQQĪ, n.d., IX, pp. 8ff.

[57] The use of past tense in this verse in no way contradicts this interpretation; as the commentators remind us, it is normal for the Qur'an to use the past tense in reference to events not taking place during human history, since they have already occurred in the divine present.

[58] KALĀBĀDHĪ, 1981, pp. 72-73.

[59] Other verses raise the same interpretive problems; e.g. Qur'an 10:94, 40:55, 47:19; on this subject, cf. *Shifā'*, 2nd part, p. 99.

[60] *Al-khitāb lahu wa l-murād ghayruhu* (cf. 'IYĀD, n.d., 2nd part, pp. 97, 157; TUSTARĪ, 2002, p. 116; 'ABD AL-QĀDIR AL-JAZĀ'IRĪ, 1966, I, p. 445).

Chapter Four

"Indeed We have granted you a clear victory" [1]

"MY MERCY EMBRACES ALL THINGS" [2]

We are indebted to Hakīm Tirmidhī for the text of the *Futūhāt* where Ibn Arabī asserts that the divine pardon promised in the second verse of Sura *al-Fath* is universal [3]. In the passage in question, the Andalusian master is proposing an answer to the question raised three centuries earlier by the author of the *Khatm al-awliyā'*: "What is the meaning of the pardon God granted [specifically] to our Prophet, since elsewhere He announced that the sins of all the prophets would be forgiven?" The fact that this is the final question in Tirmidhī's mysterious "Questionnaire" (there are more than one hundred fifty questions in all [4]) was perhaps not by chance, given the serious eschatological implications of Ibn Arabī's answer [5]. We might add that the interpretation Tirmidhī proposed for the verse above is not the only interpretation that Ibn Arabī offered. Elsewhere, the Shaykh al-Akbar sees other *ishārāt* ("allusions") [6]. The point of departure for his thoughts is nevertheless always related etymologically to the verb *ghafara*, the common meaning of which is to "pardon," though in this case it means "conceal with a veil" [7]. From this perspective, Ibn Arabī remarks, the verse somewhat sets a foundation for, and guarantees, the "impeccability" of the Prophet, as the divine veil falls between him and sin, or more precisely, between him and the *state* of sin [8]. This is at least the position he takes in the *Jawāb mustaqīm*, a work whose purpose was also to respond to Tirmidhī's "Questionnaire" [9]. The answers in chapter 73 of the *Futūhāt* do not contradict those in the *Jawāb mustaqīm*, but they are often worded differently, in the sense of looking at different aspects of a particular question. Such is the case here, for example:

> A *ghafr*, etymologically speaking, is a veil [10]. God veiled off from the prophets of our world the fact that they are substitutes

57

[*nuwwāb*] for His Messenger, but He will lift the veil in the here-after, since he [the Prophet] has declared: "I will be the master of men on the Day of Resurrection" [11]. He will intercede in their favor so that they, in turn, might intercede, for his intercession will match what is required by the status of each of those for whom he intercedes.

God was thereby announcing individual pardon for the proph-ets, but a general pardon for Muhammad [12]. Now it has been established that he was freed from committing sin; as such, there would be no sin to be forgiven. Thus, the only way to think about him as having sins is if it is the *umma* being addressed, rather than him. It is just like saying [when wanting to refer to someone without using his name]: "Look over there" [13].

This is also said: "If you have doubts about what We have re-vealed, ask those who read the Book that was revealed before you" [14]. It is well known that he had no doubts about the issue here, that it was referring to those in the Community who were in doubt. Similarly, it was said: "If you associate [something with God], your works will lose value [15]," knowing that he associ-ated nothing [with God], and that the meaning of this is: this is what will happen to whoever commits "associationism" [*shirk*]. He was also told: "So that God might forgive what preceded your sin and what came after it [16]," even though he is protected from all sin. He is consequently the one to whom the statement about pardon is addressed, even though the statement con-cerned men from the time of Adam up to his day, as well as those who came later, from his time up to the Day of the Resurrection, for they all belong to his Community [*al-kull ummatuhu*]. There actually is no community that is not subject to a divine law, and we have already established, in all cases, that the law being re-ferred to is the Law of Muhammad, in respect to his being "the hidden," since he was a prophet when "Adam was still between water and clay." He is, additionally, the master of prophets and messengers, since he is "the master of men," and they are men. All this has been previously established.

Thus, by His words "So that God might forgive your sins from be-fore and those that came after," God announced to Muhammad that his mission encompassed all men, just as He has said: "And We have not sent you but to the totality of men" [17]. This does not imply that everyone should see him, for just as in the time

of his physical presence he sent ʿAlī and Muʿādh to Yemen to
spread his call, just as he sent the prophets and messengers off
to their respective communities from the moment that he became a prophet and while "Adam was between water and clay."
He thus called all men to God.

All people are thus members of his Community, from the time of
Adam to the Day of Resurrection [*al-nās ummatuhu min Ādam ilā
yawm al-qiyāma*]. God thus informed him of pardon for the sins
previously committed by men, as well as for those that would
subsequently be committed; the words were spoken to him,
though they referred to men.

God will thus pardon all, and will grant felicity to all in accord with
the global nature of His mercy, which "embraces all things" [18]
and in accord with the global nature of Muhammad's rank, as he
was sent *to all men* according to what has been put in writing. God
did not say "We sent you to this community in particular," nor did
He say "to the men of your time and all those to come, until the
Day of Resurrection." But He did inform Muhammad that he was
sent to all peoples, which includes everyone from Adam up to the
Resurrection. It is thus they who are in mind in this declaration of
divine pardon relating to sins both past and future.

This being the case, there is pardon in this lower world, pardon
in the tomb, pardon on the day of the final Gathering, and pardon in the fire, which might consist in escaping from it *or not escaping*, in which case God will put a veil over the punishment by
bestowing well-being [upon the individual damned] in the fire
allowing him to experience a certain pleasure, *such that it ends up
being punishment without pain* [19].

The idea – so forcefully expressed in this text – that divine mercy will have the final word and that, when all is said and done,
those damned to punishment will consequently experience a sort
of "felicity" (*saʿāda*) is a recurrent theme in Ibn Arabī's writings.
Needless to say, the Doctors of the Law rejected this idea; to their
minds, it was as unorthodox as it could possibly be. It also ended
up causing a certain amount of unease (an issue to be addressed
shortly) for some who claimed to be followers of the Shaykh al-
Akbar's teachings: after all, in proclaiming loud and clear that God
will pardon everyone and everything does one not run the risk of
encouraging the common believer to disrespect the Law? Ibn Arabī

was in fact himself aware that he was shining a light on serious truths, asserting that he would not have dared to do so, were he not forced to [20].

In any case, the several texts where he mentions the "felicity" that all men, without exception (ma'āl al-kull ilā l-sa'āda) [21], are sooner or later destined to experience should not allow us to forget the still greater number of those strictly observing the Law [22]. In other words, reminding us of this basic truth set forth in Revelation – according to which Divine Mercy "embraces all things" [23] – the author of the Futūhāt in no way intends to encourage laxity toward legal obligations; and even less is he wanting to downplay the seriousness of "sin." Rather, he hopes [24] by his actions to encourage his peers to desire increasing closeness to Him who said [25]: "Oh My servants, you who have transgressed at your own expense, do not lose hope in the Mercy of the Lord, for in truth the Lord pardons all sins!" [26].

Moreover, it is important to point out that, even if he is convinced that all men will end up attaining eternal salvation, Ibn Arabī is just as strongly affirming the reality of the infernal underworld and of the punishments that await its denizens [27]. Besides, the "felicity" he claims the damned will ultimately have access to is in no way comparable to what is held in store for the blessed: between the absence of suffering and beatitude stands a great abyss – the same abyss that stands between the "People of hell" and the "People of Paradise." Ibn Arabi ends up clarifying that there is one kind of torment that will never completely disappear for those who are damned: the fear of suffering again [28].

The fact remains that for Ibn Arabī, "apocatastasis" – the "reestablishment," the "restoration" of everything, to borrow an expression from the New Testament [29] – is ineluctable, and he never misses an opportunity to make his case, complete with supporting arguments. A look at his writings on the subject shows these arguments taking shape around three major themes: the infinity of Divine mercy, the "original nature" (fitra) of man, and the universality of the Prophet's soteriological role. Each of these has its scriptural foundation in one or several Qur'anic verses – as well as in numerous hadiths – which Ibn Arabī unsurprisingly proposes should be understood literally.

This adherence to the literal reading of the Divine Word moreover allows him to avoid the primary objection of the ulama, who maintain that the Qur'an asserts repeatedly that the "People of hell" *will remain* in Gehenna forever:

> Each of the two abodes of the afterlife will be filled, for God has told us that He will fill them and that the stay in each will be eternal. But there is no text [*nass*] *about the eternity of punishment being pain* [30].

> [...] This is one of the most complex questions that there are on this Path. Indeed, God said that His mercy came before His wrath, [...] it will take over the world in both abodes, because of God's generosity, "and that is not hard for God [31]." Thus, even surrounded by flames, [the damned] will experience a certain well-being [*na'īm*], albeit without escaping them. Thus His words will be fulfilled: "My mercy preceded my wrath [32]," as will His statement: "I will fill Gehenna with jinn and with men, both together [33]" and also His affirmation that "My mercy embraces all things [34]." I have taken the veil off something in this regard without having a choice, but have done so in accord with divine command, which demanded that it be exposed; I was like the man who is forced to make the choice he makes [35].

> [...] At the same time, the People of the unveiling diverge in their opinions regarding this issue: will the damned suffer punishment for an eternity without end, or will they perhaps experience some well-being [*na'īm*] in the abode of damnation, in which case punishment will cease after a certain period of time? They agree on the fact that they will not escape and that they will remain there forever, for each of the two abodes will be filled, and the causes of their torment will vary on the outside; this fact is ineluctable. But – and this is their point of disagreement – once their pain has taken from them the amount of punishment they owed, they will experience an inner pleasure.

> [...] When the measure [due for the penalty they owe] has reached its term, well-being [*na'īm*] will be accorded them *in the fire*, such that, if they entered Paradise, they would suffer because the constitution that God gave them is incompatible with [the abode of Paradise]; so they will experience pleasure in finding themselves in fire and in the cold [...] [36].

If they left hell, those who reside there would suffer from being separated from what they are accustomed to, because God created them with a constitution appropriate for this [infernal] place.

[...] On the other hand, God is "the most Merciful of the Merciful [37]," as He Himself has said. There are in our midst – among those whom God has created to be inclined toward mercy – those who feel compassion toward God's servants to the point that, if God allowed them to reign, they would have punishment cease throughout the universe because it is mercy that governs their hearts. However, such beings – my peers and I – are but mere creatures subject to passions and desires. Now, God has said that He was "the most Merciful of the Merciful." There is no doubt that He is the more merciful toward His creatures than we; and since we have observed such compassion within ourselves, how could punishment last for eternity, if one of God's attributes is total Mercy? [38]

As terrible, as numerous as a man's sins might be, they nevertheless do come to an end, and the expiation they correspondingly call for should, necessarily, also end, by virtue of the compassion that God, the Qur'an tells us, has imposed upon Himself [39]. For all this, Ibn Arabī does not question the eternal and definitive nature of hell as far as this concerns the *ahl al-nār* – a Qur'anic term referring justly to those sinners who, in contrast to others for whom time in hell will be temporary, are doomed never to leave Gehenna. Nor does he say that the environment in hell will be modified: fire, cold, scorpions, and all the rest will remain forever. What could not be perpetual is suffering caused by the elements; a time will thus come when they will become a source of well-being and satisfaction for those in hell, and this because God, in His infinite mercy, will have endowed them with a constitution specifically appropriate for this milieu [40].

"AM I NOT YOUR LORD" [41]

Ibn Arabī's second argument for a universal apocatastasis focuses on the idea of *fitra* [42], man's "original nature." Like most Qur'anic commentators, he posits a relationship between the verse where the word appears – in this case, "Set your face to the service of religion, as a pure devotee (*hanīfan*), according to the original nature in which He created mankind. There is no altering of God's creation" [43], and the previously-noted Sura *al-Aʿraf*, which refers to the Primordial Pact (*mīthāq*) made in pre-eternity between God and mankind: "And when, from the loins of Adam's sons, your Lord took their offspring and made them bear witness against themselves: 'Am I not your Lord?' they replied 'Yes, surely'" [44].

At that point of departure for their spiritual destiny, all men thus pledged allegiance to the One God. For Ibn Arabī, this solemn recognition of divine sovereignty and, consequently, of one's own nature as *'abd*, "servant," specifically constitutes the "original nature" with which man was endowed at the time of his creation.

Up to this point Ibn Arabī's interpretation is, *mutatis mutandis*, very much in line with that of other commentators. But it then veers off on one key point: while others consider this *fitra* to be modifiable depending on the choices individuals make after their birth as physical beings – regarding adherence to monotheism, or not – the Shaykh al-Akbar, on the other hand, believes *fitra* to be *absolutely unalterable*: the end of the verse states that there is "No change in God's creation":

> This [verse 30:30] is good news coming from God, announcing that He created us with a nature patterned on this [primordial] recognition of divine sovereignty. Nothing appearing in certain individuals to be "associationism" (*shirk*) is able to change this recognition, since God has denied the possibility of their making such a change. They remain in complete conformity to their "original nature," and associationists will return to it on the Day of Judgment. [...] This is thus good news in their regard, announcing that they will return to Mercy; even if they remain in hell, it will be because it is a place to abide, not because it is a place of suffering [45].

Whatever he does to attempt to make it disappear, man is incapable of escaping his servitude, as it is his ineluctable ontological status. From this perspective, like it or not, he remains inextricably tied by the pledge of allegiance he made at the time of the Covenant – a pledge that, in return, guaranteed his obtaining eternal salvation at the end of time:

> When the time of sanctions for good and evil actions arrives for the "People of Paradise" and the "People of Hell," they will still have the reward that is their due, the reward for "worship" [*al-'ibāda*] owed to the blessed, and the reward for "servitude" [*ubūdiyya*] owed to those who are damned. And this is a reward that never ceases, because of the infinite and all-encompassing mercy of God.

> Actually, reprobates have never ceased contemplating their "servitude," even if they strived for sovereignty, for they knew,

deep inside, that they were lying. [...] They will thus reap the fruit of their assent for having said "Yes, certainly" [balā]. They are like those who convert after apostasy. [...] The authority of that "Yes, certainly" remains forever with them, from that moment [of uttering the words] to the end of time [...] [46].

The "original nature" according to which God created all men is that they worship only Him; and this "original nature" relating to recognizing Divine Uniqueness continues to be theirs. [...] *For the worshiper worships only God in that to which he attributes divinity.* We thus see that the recognition of the Divine Uniqueness proclaimed by men at the time of the Pact lasts forever, just as they cannot escape their "original nature" [47].

In other words, *shirk* - "associationism," a serious sin in Islam - is an "accident" ('arad), it is incidental, and everything connected to it is bound to disappear, leaving the one Principle in its place:

Everything incidental will necessarily cease to be and any status it holds will also cease with its disappearance; authority then returns to the Principle, and the Principle requires felicity; all will thus return to felicity, if God so wishes [48].

[...] Glory be to God, Who created the world for felicity, not for damnation! Damnation is incidental; it will take place, and then cease to exist, for God did not create the world but for Himself. [...] God will thus be merciful to all, and that is the meaning of "My mercy embraces all things" [49].

"AND WE HAVE NOT SENT YOU BUT AS A MERCY FOR THE WORLDS" [50]

Such as it was worded in the text of the *Futūhāt* in the beginning of this chapter, the answer to the last of Tirmidhī's questions - "What does the pardon that God granted to our Prophet mean?" - brings to the fore a third argument regarding Ibn Arabī's teachings on universal salvation. What we see is the Shaykh al-Akbar establishing a cause-and-effect relationship between the Prophet and the felicity that will be bestowed, permanently, upon all of humanity - a bestowal where the Prophet appears to be the instrument. The idea of the "Muhammadan Reality" plays an essential role here: because the Muhammadan Spirit has been fulfilling its magisterium throughout the whole of human history, the Prophet's mission encompasses the human race in its entirety. Consequently, all men - from the first to the last - belong to his Community. He who belongs to Muhammad's Community would, of course, be incapable of incurring divine wrath.

This theme of Muhammad's role as savior also shows up in a *Futūhāt* passage where Ibn Arabī addresses another of Tirmidhī's questions, this one regarding the meaning of the hadith: "The People of My House (*ahlu baytī*) are a safeguard for My Community" [51]. He immediately mentions another hadith, where the Prophet is said to have stated: "Salmān is one of us, one of the People of the House" [52]. Even though he is considered to be one of the most illustrious of the Companions, Salmān al-Fārisī – a Persian by birth, as his name states – is in no way one of the Prophet's relatives. In other words, those belonging to the "family" include not only his closest blood relatives, but also those who are related to him through spiritual lineage [53], just as "his Community" is not restricted to members of his tribe. This interpretation leads him to the following conclusions:

> [...] Not a single one of those to whom the Prophet was sent who affirmed the oneness of God will remain in the fire any longer. Better still, no man toward whom he was sent will continue to be damned [for eternity]; even if he should remain in the fire, it would become, for him, "freshness and peace" [54], by virtue of the blessing attached to "the People of the House." [...]

> On the Day of Resurrection, men will thus be under blessed protection as "People of the House" – those to whom he was sent. Blessed, thus, is this Community, for if God looks upon the "House" in the hidden sense of the word [where it denotes spiritual rather than physical lineage] and given that all previous Law is Muhammad's Law [...], Muhammad's *umma* then stretches from Adam up to the last human being to exist. From this point of view, *each and every one belongs to the Community of Muhammad; each and every one will thus receive the blessing of the "People of the House," and consequently all will enjoy happiness.* Do you not see that he [the Prophet] said "I will be at the head *of mankind* on the Day of Resurrection" and not "the head of my [historical] Community"[55]?

Ibn Arabī saw scriptural proof that the Prophet's soteriological role unambiguously included everyone, whether they were Muslims or not, believers or not, in the verse that proclaimed: "And we have sent you only as a mercy for *the worlds* [56]":

God sent the most perfect of messengers, him whose authority is the most eminent, whose mission is the most global, "as a mercy for the worlds," without specifying any particular world. Therefore, both he who obeys and he who disobeys, he who believes and he who does not, he who affirms the Oneness of God and he who associates [other gods] with him are included in the word referring to the world [57].

[...] His mercy encompasses the world, for it is by His mercy that he was sent, because God said: "And we have sent you only as a mercy for the worlds." God was thus announcing that He had sent him so that he might be a mercy for the world, without singling out one world rather than another [58].

Incidentally, the author of the *Futūhāt* was not the first to highlight the general scope that "for the worlds" included. In his *tafsīr*, Sulamī cited Abū l-Husayn al-Fārisī (d. 370/981), who was speaking similarly [59], as well as a sentence by Abū Bakr al-Abharī (d. 330/941) claiming that the entirety of the Prophet's being was a mercy for creatures [60]. Similarly, Abū l-ʿAbbās al-Mursī (d. 686/1287) was maintaining, a few decades after Ibn Arabi, that: "All the prophets were created out of mercy. Our Prophet is the very essence of mercy [*ʿayn al-rahma*]" [61].

It is not until much later, however, that we find the most complete, and the most original, doctrinal explanation of this issue, in ʿAbd al-Karīm al-Jīlī. Though he belongs to what has come to be called the "Akbarian school," Jīlī never had problems distancing himself from Ibn Arabi when he disagreed with him. But on the issue of the universal mercy of the Prophet, his position was very much in line with that of the Shaykh al-Akbar:

God said: "We have sent you only as a mercy for the worlds." Know that this mercy is the mercy that embraces all beings [*al-mawjūdāt*], and it is to it that his words "My mercy embraces all things" refer. This means that Muhammad embraces everything that can be called a "thing," whether it be of a higher nature or lower nature [62].

Know that there are two kinds of mercy, one of which is specific and the other general. Specific mercy refers to that granted by God to His servants at specific moments, and *general mercy is the "Reality" of Muhammad, and it is through this that God bestows mercy upon the realities of things.* [...] This is why the first thing that God created was Muhammad's spirit, as well as why this is mentioned in Jābir's hadith [63], so that through him He might show mercy to the creatures and fashion them according to the prophetic model [*nuskha*].

[...] This is why His mercy preceded His wrath, for the entire universe is in the image of the "beloved" [the Prophet] and the "beloved" is an object of mercy [*marhūm*]. The status [*hukm*] of mercy thus belongs to the order of the necessary, while that of divine wrath belongs to the incidental [64].

It thus appears, from all that we have mentioned, that if the Prophet had not existed, not one thing among the beings would know its Lord; even more, the universe itself would not exist, for God did not create the universe but for one reason: that He might know it. [...]

The Prophet thus obtained the abode of intercession [*al-wasīla*] in the hereafter precisely because the creatures succeed in knowing God only through His intermediary, just as it is through his intervention that they were brought into being [65].

[The Prophet] is thus that by which the universe lives; he is the supreme mercy [*al-rahma al-ʿuzmā*] that embraces all beings [...], which is why God said in reference to him "We have not sent you but as a mercy," without specifying that the mercy concerns the believer rather than the unbeliever, the blessed rather than the damned; his mercy encompasses the entirety of existence, the lower and the higher [66].

It should be added that Jīlī shows himself to be just as formal as Ibn Arabī when it comes to the suffering that is inflicted on the damned not being eternal:

Do you not see that He told me "My mercy embraces all things," and not "My wrath embraces all things" for He gave existence to things through pure mercy, and it is for this reason also that anger cannot exert its status indefinitely. The secret in this is that mercy is an attribute of Essence; this is not the case for wrath [...].

Know that fire, in that it belongs to the incidental, can disappear – the opposite is impossible – and its disappearance means nothing other than that it will cease to burn; and when it ceases to burn, the angels watching over it will leave, ceding their place to angels in charge of well-being [*naʿīm*]. [...] Thus that which was a blaze will be transmuted, into well-being, just as what happened in the story of Abraham when God said to the fire: "Be freshness and peace upon Abraham [...]" [67]

Jīlī is addressing an issue here that we saw Ibn ʿArabī address previously. His wording is almost identical to a passage from the *Fuṣūṣ al-ḥikam* [68], Ibn ʿArabī's magnum opus that generated so many commentaries among his "heirs." It is remarkable in this regard that so many of these followers – some of whom are among the most eminent representatives of the Shaykh al-Akbar's school – tend to limit themselves to brief paraphrases of the passage in question, without adding their own opinions. Such was the case for Qayṣarī (d. 751/1350), for example, as it was for Nābulusī (d. 1143/1731), and Sāʾin al-Dīn Turkah (d. 830/1427) [69]. Qāshānī (d. 730/1330) [70] and Jandī (d. c.700/1300) [71] do not disagree with the Shaykh's point of view, but are clearly ill at ease in justifying it. Bālī Efendī (d. 960/1553) ended up accusing his predecessors of twisting Ibn ʿArabī's words, maintaining that the latter never claimed that those in hell would cease to suffer [72], while Muṣṭafā Bālī Zāde (d. 1069/1658) attempted to adjust what Ibn ʿArabī was saying by explaining that the damned would suffer eternally in body, but not in spirit [73].

Emir ʿAbd al-Qādir al-Jazāʾirī, on the other hand, unreservedly subscribes to Ibn ʿArabī's doctrine of apocatastasis, and on this question (as on many others [74]) it is he, among the Shaykh al-Akbar's disciples, who most faithfully gives an account of the teaching. One example is chapter 205 of the *Mawāqif*, dedicated to commentary on the first verses of Sura 48: "Certainly, We have given you a stunning victory. So that God might pardon you for those sins of yours which were committed before, and those which ere committed later." If at first he limits himself to explicating the interpretation offered by several mystics – where the pardon at issue is for Muhammad's Community (in the common and narrow sense of the word *umma*) – the emir unhesitatingly offers another point of view, the universalist perspective seen by Ibn ʿArabī:

It is legitimate to think of this "stunning victory" as a more general, more comprehensive one, meaning that God informed His Messenger (may Grace and Peace be upon Him) about the general and global nature of divine mercy benefitting all of Adam's sons, once divine wrath has fulfilled its rightful duties, since all of Adam's sons are the Prophet's Community, and the messengers of God are – from the first among them to the last – his substitutes and his lieutenants [75].

No less in line with Ibn Arabī's teachings is this *Mawāqif* passage regarding the fate reserved for the condemned:

> [...] The fact that Gehenna is the abode of the damned, a place they will inhabit for an eternal stay – for those who are Gehenna's true denizens will never be released – does not imply that the suffering inflicted upon them will last for an eternity without end.

> [...] His Mercy for the "People of Hell" [...] will be that He will confer upon them a constitution such that they will take pleasure from what made them suffer and will experience well-being due to what had [previously] inflicted their pain. [...] Such that if they entered Paradise they would suffer because of their constitutions.

> [...] The "men of God," meaning the men of unveiling and realization, are unanimous in saying that the abode of the damned is eternal (just as is that of the blessed), and what is reported regarding some of them or what is found in their writings regarding the disappearance and the cessation of fire should not be understood from an outside perspective. What they are referring to is the cessation of torment and suffering inflicted upon those who are there; [...] their abode is their abode; they will not leave it nor will they ever get out. [...] *Just as the Men of God are unanimous in maintaining the universality of mercy and the obtaining of rest and well-being by those condemned* [76].

What we see here are the main themes in Ibn Arabī's doctrine of apocatastasis: the eternity of one's time in hell but the non-eternity of the suffering inflicted upon the damned, felicity in flames by virtue of a constitution appropriate for the "People of Hell," and so forth. Nothing up to this point is really surprising, so where did emir ʿAbd al-Qādir al-Jazāʾirī get the idea that there was consensus among Muslim spiritual thinkers regarding the idea that the damned would, in the end, find eternal salvation? As we saw earlier, Ibn Arabī himself, in the *Futūhāt*, mentions disagreement among teachers on this issue.

What we do have is this: in one passage from the *Fusūs* – where he mentions, albeit briefly, the question of salvation for those condemned to hell and the opinion that prevailed among Muslim spiritual writers on the subject – Ibn Arabī offers an observation similar to the emir's:

> Not one of the men of [spiritual] knowledge who have had the truth regarding this matter revealed to them has categorically asserted that those who are condemned will not, in their infernal abode, experience a well-being that is appropriate for them, either through the cessation of the suffering they endure – which would thus constitute the well-being in question – or through their experiencing a different sense of well-being, as is the case for the People of Paradise [77].

This wording is certainly much narrower and more nuanced than the language used by ʿAbd al-Qādir: here it is no longer "men of God" in general, but rather those men of God who have had a revelation regarding the matter. All the same, if we go back to what we know at present about *their writings*, we still must admit that among Sunni spiritual writers who preceded Ibn Arabī, we are hard pressed to find a doctrinal statement regarding apocatastasis, with the exception of Tirmidhī, whom Geneviève Gobillot has shown to have envisioned the possibility of a happy outcome for those condemned to hell [78].

In fact, in the *Mawāqif* chapter where he addresses the beginning of Sura 48 – which, following Ibn Arabī's example, he interprets as a promise of divine pardon granted to all mankind without exception – the emir mentions three proponents, and only three, of the theory [79]: Ibn Arabī, ʿAlī Wafā (who was, like his father before him, the eminent head of a sizable brotherhood based in Egypt, and whose writings were permeated with key ideas regarding Ibn Arabī's initiatory and metaphysical teachings [80]), and Jīlī.

However, given the near total absence of documentary information, might we be obliged to conclude that all the countless spiritual teachers preceding Ibn Arabī denied the possibility that divine wrath toward the People of Hell would come to an end, while at the same time so many of their works so incessantly dwelled on God's love for men and His inexhaustible mercy?

The answer is, probably not. It would appear to me that the same is true for the idea of *shumūl al-rahma*, as well as that of *shumūl al-umma*: Ibn Arabī was certainly the first to offer a solid and structured doctrinal foundation for the idea that the human community in its entirety constitutes the Community of Muhammad. He did not invent it out of the blue, however. Seeds of the idea existed in the mystical concept of *nūr muhammadī*, which we have seen had been around since the earliest days of Islam. One anecdote in Ibn Arabī's *Futūhāt* is especially enlightening in this regard – one concerning Tustarī's spiritual biography [81]. I refer to the episode during which the saint, when confronted by Satan, found himself forced to retreat: at the end of a long and bitter discussion dealing precisely with the question of whether damnation was to last for all eternity, the Evil One got the better of his adversary by making the point that, to the extent that divine mercy encompasses "all things," he – being a "thing" himself – is assured of equal benefit. Tustarī ended his account stating that in the absence of formal scriptural proof regarding the matter, he preferred to reserve judgment.

In other words, Tustarī *did not express an opinion* about the possibility, or the impossibility, of universal redemption. Massignon – based on his reading of this account – categorizes him as a latitudinarian [82]. The conclusion appears somewhat hasty to me, to say the least, and it is not one shared by Kamāl Jaʿfar in his analysis of the anecdote [83].

The author of *The Passion of al-Hallâj* actually also accuses imam Jaʿfar and Ibn ʿAtāʾ of the same universalist teachings about salvation, based on their statements regarding the pre-eternal "Muhammadan Light" [84]. If it does happen to be true that the *nūr muhammadī* doctrine is capable of spilling over into a broader idea about the salvific role of the Prophet, nothing has been seen in their writings that leads one to think they formally professed such beliefs. Better to be prudent until more solid evidence is available.

Conversely, Massignon was convinced that Hallāj – who was Tustarī's disciple and shared his thinking regarding the pre-existence of the Prophet – supported the irrevocable nature of God's pronouncement regarding the damned, despite the fact that he had no tangible evidence to offer.

In fact, if we look carefully at the texts where he asserts that Hallāj ruled out the possibility of any form of salvation for the damned [85], we are forced to admit that the only argument Massignon offers is second hand testimony. It is true that in another passage from his monumental study [86], *The Passion*'s author also refers to a section of the *Tawāsīn* where Hallāj, in regard to Satan, declares: "He tied himself to damnation for the post-eternity of all post-eternities" [87]. The sentences in question were not probably Hallāj's however – they did not appear in Massignon's first Arabic edition of the text [88] – but rather came from Ruzbehān Baqlī (d. 606/1209) who, this time, was refusing to believe that Satan could be saved [89].

This brings us to the famous testimony that Massignon offers on numerous occasions [90], and which leads him to believe in the "orthodoxy" of Hallāj's teachings regarding the fate of the damned [91]. At issue is an account in Ismāʿīl Haqqī's *Rūḥ al-bayān* [92] which is made by the author to sound like an autobiographical text by Ibn Arabī – though neither Massignon nor any scholar after him has yet found its original source – an account that Haqqī offers a different version of elsewhere, this time attributing it to Abū l'Hasan Shādhilī [93]. Whatever the case, the text says that Hallāj incurred the Prophet's anger *post mortem,* by criticizing the fact that he restricted his intercession to the sole benefit of "sinners in my Community."

Even if we admit that judgment might be passed regarding al-Hallāj's eschatological beliefs based solely on this single indirect testimony, two comments are in order. First, what is at issue here is not the fate of the damned strictly speaking, but rather the Prophet's ability to intercede. Second, Massignon appears to have forgotten that even if the theologians reject latitudinarianism, they are in no way challenging the absolutely universal nature of the Prophet's intercession on the Day of Judgment: this has been clearly established by numerous hadiths that deal with the Prophet's *shafāʿa* ("intercession"): hadiths recognized as authentic by the ulama's own criteria.

In this regard, it should be said that according to these hadiths, the Prophet will not intercede just once, but numerous times and at different stages of the Last Judgment [94]. *One* of these interventions will concern the Muslim Community specifically, according to several hadiths – and here we see *umma* used only in the narrow sense of the term, namely the one alluded to at the end of the story reported by Ismāʿīl Haqqī, where the Prophet is said to have declared "My intercession will be for the great sinners of my Community" [95]. The question has also arisen regarding the specific moment that this intercession, for Muslims alone, is to take place.

This cannot be referring to the first intercession, also called *al-shafāʿa al-ʿuzmā* ("the supreme intercession"), the one taking place immediately after the Resurrection and which, with no doubt whatsoever, involves the entirety of humanity. Terrified at the prospect of appearing before God, men call upon Adam to intervene on their behalf. However, the father of the human race prefers to stand down, given the sin he committed in paradise, and he suggests they see Noah. Noah also declines and encourages them to check with Abraham. The men end up going from one prophet to another until they get to Muhammad, who is willing to take on the task. The Prophet showers God with all the praises he can think of on the spot [96], and then begins the cycle of intercessions by arranging for all beings capable of interceding to do so: angels, prophets, men, and so forth. It is in this way, says Ibn Arabī, that the Prophet will be the "master of men" on the Day of Judgment, as the power he holds will be shown at this time [97].

These hadiths assert that the Prophet, later on, will arrange for seventy thousand believers from "his Community" to be exempt from the "accounting" (*hisāb*) and led straight to heaven. After this, he will intervene similarly so that a certain number of sinners, having earned the privilege, will also be exempted from punishment. And then, in a final stage, the Prophet will intercede in favor of the *jahannamiyyūn*: those condemned to hell whose stay there will be limited in time, precisely because of his intervention. According to the ulama, this is how the salvific mission of the Prophet will be accomplished.

Ibn Arabī does not happen to hold this view. His explanation is that at the Last Judgment the Prophet will limit himself to acting in favor of those whose state deserves the benefit of divine mercy immediately. Out of respect for divine majesty, he will temporarily refrain from addressing the cases of the others, until such time as God shows Himself through some attribute other than wrath. It is at that point that his merciful role will fully be shown, because thanks to him, God will forgive those who are damned, either by releasing them from Gehenna (in the case of the *jahannamiyyūn*), or (in the case of the "People of Hell") by granting them felicity in their infernal abode [98].

This is how the "stunning victory" promised to the Prophet will unfold.

Notes

[1] Qur'an 48:1.
[2] Qur'an 7:156
[3] The first meaning of the word *fath* is "opening"; this Sura thus is closely re-

lated to the Qur'an's first Sura, *Al-Fātiha*, "That which opens." It should also be noted that – according to a note in CHODKIEWICZ, 2005, c, note 6 – this Sura, 48, has three hundred and sixty words, the same number as both Ibn Arabī's date of birth and the number of chapters in the *Futūhāt*.

[4] This set of questions appears in TIRMIDHĪ, 1965, pp. 142-325; ID., 1992 (b), pp. 20-29 (cf. also RADTKE & O'KANE, 1996, pp. 71-86, for the English translation). Note that the numbering and occasionally the wording of questions sometimes differ from one edition to another.

[5] IBN ARABĪ, 1911, II, pp. 138-139.

[6] Cf., for example, *ibid.*, I, p. 622, II, p. 359, III, p. 153.

[7] See below, note 10.

[8] This interpretation will be repeated by 'Abd al-Dā'im al-Birmāwī (d. 831/1428); cf. ZURQĀNĪ, 1996, IX, p. 21.

[9] Cf. IBN ARABĪ, 1965, pp. 142-325, for this "Questionnaire" as well as for the answers given in the *Futūhāt*; the *Jawāb mustaqīm* was written in 603 A.H. (cf. YAHIA, 1964, R.G., 177), and thus at a time when composition of the *Futūhat* was well underway.

[10] A number of words relating to the idea of pardon are derived from the root *gh/f/r*, notably the verb *ghafara*, "to pardon," used in the verse in question. However, as is often the case when he comments on Revelation, Ibn Arabī's support comes from the first meaning of the word *ghafr*, which properly speaking is "veil."

[11] Cf. WENSINCK, 1936-1969, III, p. 17.

[12] Ibn Arabī appears here to be referring to the fact that each prophet can intercede for his own community, while Muhammad is interceding for all communities and for all men, as he attempts to show in the text that follows.

[13] Ibn Arabī cites this proverb on numerous occasions; it even serves for the title of chapter 359 in IBN ARABĪ, 1911, III, p. 269; cf. also *ibid.*, p. 185; ID., 1948 (c), ch. XLV.

[14] Qur'an 10:94.

[15] Qur'an 39:65.

[16] Qur'an 48:2.

[17] Qur'an 34:28.

[18] Qur'an 7:156.

[19] IBN ARABĪ, 1911, II, pp. 138-139 (italics mine).

[20] IBN ARABĪ, 1911, II, p. 224.

[21] *Ibid.*, p. 213.

[22] A number of works have pointed out the extreme importance Ibn Arabī places on observing the Law in the path to sainthood, e.g. CHODKIEWICZ, 1994 (a), ch. 5.

[23] Qur'an 7:156.

[24] In this regard, cf. IBN ARABĪ, 1911, I, p. 708, which reports a vision in which God commands him to make His mercy known.

[25] Qur'an 39:53.

[26] On interpretation of this verse, cf. IBN ARABĪ, 1911, III, p. 148.

[27] Cf. especially chapter 61 of the *Futūhāt* (ibid., I, pp. 297-301).

[28] *Ibid.*, I, p. 169.

[29] Acts 3:21.

[30] The same statement in IBN ARABĪ, 1911, I, p. 164 (italics mine).

[31] Qurʾan 35:17.

[32] This hadith appears in a number of collections (cf. WENSINCK, 1936-1969, II, p. 239).

[33] Qurʾan 11:119.

[34] Qurʾan 7:156.

[35] IBN ARABĪ, 1911, II, p. 673.

[36] *Ibid.*, p. 648 (italics mine).

[37] An expression appearing in the famous hadith about intercession: on the many variants of this hadith, cf. NABHĀNĪ, 1996 (b), pp. 95ff.

[38] IBN ARABĪ, 1911, III, p. 25.

[39] Qurʾan 6:54.

[40] IBN ARABĪ, 1911, II, p. 207.

[41] Qurʾan 7:172.

[42] On the concept of *fitra*, cf. the excellent study by GOBILLOT, 2000.

[43] Qurʾan 30:30.

[44] Qurʾan 7:172.

[45] IBN ARABĪ, 1911, II, pp. 534-535.

[46] *Ibid.*, pp. 212-213.

[47] *Ibid.*, III, p. 24 (italics mine).

[48] *Ibid.*, II, p. 213.

[49] *Ibid.*, p. 220.

[50] Qurʾan 21:107.

[51] IBN ARABĪ, 1911, II, pp. 126-127. On Ibn Arabī's interpretation of this hadith, cf. *infra*, the beginning of chapter 8.

[52] On this subject, cf. *EI2*, "Salmān al-Fārisī"; MASSIGNON, 1969, I, pp. 453-455.

[53] This theme is discussed *infra*, in chapter 8.

[54] An allusion to the verse (Qurʾan 21:69) reporting the fire into which Abraham was thrown miraculously changing its nature such that it became "coolness and peace."

[55] IBN ARABĪ, 1911, II, pp. 126-127 (italics mine).

[56] Qurʾan 21:107 (italics mine).

[57] IBN ARABĪ, 1911, III, p. 567.

[58] *Ibid.*, p. 143.

[59] SULAMĪ, 1986, p. 97.

[60] ID., 2001, II, p. 17.

[61] IBN ʿATĀʾ ALLĀH, 1992, p. 62.

[62] JĪLĪ, 2004, p. 17.

[63] See above, p. 35 (italics mine).

[64] *Ibid.*, pp. 17-18.

[65] *Ibid.*, p. 20.

[66] *Ibid.*, p. 127.

[67] ID., 1970, 2nd part, p. 184.

[68] IBN ARABĪ, 1980, p. 169 (cf. also *ibid*, p. 114).

[69] For example, NĀBULUSĪ, 1304 A.H., p. 197; QAYSARĪ, 1380 A.H., p. 314; SĀʾIN

AL-DĪN TURKAH, 1420 A.H., pp. 697-698.

[70] QAYSARĪ, 1380 A.H., p. 257.

[71] JANDĪ, 1982, p. 565.

[72] BĀLĪ EFENDĪ, 1309 A.H., p. 139.

[73] MUSTAFĀ BĀLĪ ZĀDE, 2002, pp. 238-241.

[74] CHODKIEWICZ, 1986, p. 175; ID., 1982, pp. 15-38.

[75] A large part of this passage was seriously damaged in the Damascus edition (ʿABD AL-QĀDIR AL-JAZĀʾIRĪ, 1966, I, p. 445); we have here relied on the text from the manuscript in Algiers, 1983, I, folio 133; Reverend M. Lagarde does not appear to have been aware of this lacuna when doing his translation (ID. 2000, I, p. 589).

[76] ID., 1966, pp. 1060-1061 (italics mine).

[77] IBN ARABĪ, 1980, p. 114.

[78] GOBILLOT, 2002 (a).

[79] ʿABD AL-QĀDIR AL-JAZĀʾIRĪ, 1966, I, p. 446.

[80] McGREGOR, 2004.

[81] IBN ARABĪ, 1911, II, p. 662, III, p. 466. This anecdote was also reported in IBN AL-ʿIMĀD, 1979, II, p. 184, with the claim that it came from Ibn Arabī's *Bulghat al-ghawwās*; cf. also SHAʿRĀNĪ, 1985, 2nd part, pp. 4-6.

[82] MASSIGNON, 1975, p. 325, 376; ID., 1968, p. 296.

[83] KAMĀL JAʿFAR, 1974, p. 344.

[84] MASSIGNON, 1975, III, p. 217.

[85] *Ibid.*, pp. 176, 217.

[86] *Ibid.*, p. 176.

[87] *Ibid.*, p. 333.

[88] HALLĀJ, 1913, p. 13. This fragment is also missing in the edition of the Persian text by H. Corbin, in RUZBEHĀN BAQLĪ, 1966.

[89] This point was discussed at length in a note by AWN, 1983, p. 128.

[90] For example, MASSIGNON, 1975, II, pp. 347, 418; ID., 1969, II, pp. 52, 351, 559.

[91] Massignon does not hide the fact that he considers the universalist doctrine of salvation to be an aberration.

[92] HAQQĪ, n.d., X, p. 456.

[93] *Ibid.*, I, pp. 248. On the problems that arise from these two texts, cf. CHODKIE-WICZ, 1986, pp. 166-168. To the discrepancies that Chodkiewicz notes in the two accounts, we might add that Ismāʿil Haqqī claims to base the story about Shādhilī on Rāghib Isfahānī's *Muhādarāt*, though Isfahānī died long before Shādhilī (in 502 A.H. at the latest; cf. *EI2, s.v.*). Whatever the case, the account in question is not from the *Muhādarāt*. It should be added that NABHĀNĪ, 1998, II, pp. 519-531, recorded ʿAbd Allāh Mīrghanī al-Mahjūb's text (d. 1207/1793) where the account is present – Mīrghanī claims to have received it from one of his teachers – according to which Abū l-Hasan al-Shādhilī was present at a general meeting of prophets gathering to intercede on behalf of al-Hallāj, who had been disrespectful toward the Prophet.

[94] NABHĀNĪ, 1966 (b), pp. 94-102; ʿIYĀD, n.d., 1st part, pp. 206-228; QASTALLĀNĪ, 1996, XII, pp. 314-414. The number of intercessions attributed to the Prophet vary from five to six, depending on the author.

[95] WENSINCK, 1936-1969, III, p. 151.
[96] This event refers to the "station of praise" (*al-maqām al-mahmūd*) that is mentioned in Qur'an 17:79. For the interpretation of the *maqām mahmūd* that Ibn Arabī offers, cf. CHODKIEWICZ, 1997, pp. 45-58.
[97] IBN ARABĪ, 1911, I, p. 313.
[98] *Ibid.*, II, p. 127, question 150, III, p. 25.

Chapter Five

"For you there is an excellent model in God's Messenger" [1]

"The Qur'an was his nature" [2]

From the earliest days of his mission, Muhammad's behavior – in all circumstances of daily life – was seen by his Companions to be the norm par excellence. It was exemplary by necessity, in light of the statement in Revelation: "For you, there is an excellent model (*uswa*) in God's Messenger." The first Muslims thus took to heart the practice of learning from the Prophet's behavior. They never failed to ask him, or to ask those closest to him, either how they might most faithfully behave in one circumstance or another, or more generally about how they should live.

When they no longer had access to the Messenger's physical presence, later generations did all they could to preserve the memory of his Sunna, his "conduct," which they did by collecting hadiths – eye witness accounts that supposedly could be traced back to the first generation of Muslims, reporting what the Prophet and his Companions said and did – and ended up collecting them in a substantial corpus of which six books are reputed to be canonical. A brief glance at the table of contents for any of these thick volumes suffices to convince one that – if the place given to "ritual works" (the '*ibadāt*) is substantial – the place held by everything relating to "social behavior" (*mu'āmalāt*) and, more broadly, everything related to what one does in daily life (like eating, drinking, sleeping and so forth) is far from negligible.

The zeal exhibited by Muslims striving to preserve, in as much detail as possible, the ways and customs of the Prophet during the first three centuries – and, more generally, the attachment believers had, and still have today, to observing a Sunna that holds as much legal authority as the Qur'an – are off-putting (even irritating) to Western observers like Goldziher. In his monumental study on Muslim Traditions, he decried "those Sunna fanatics working to track down hadiths about the daily habits of the prophet and his Companions so they can then find the chance to put these behaviors into practice and save them from oblivion" [3]. It is undeniable that desire to imitate the Prophet in every possible way has occasionally led the ulama into trivial *quaestiones disputatae* – "Precisely how long was the Prophet's beard?" – and even into violent polemics, most notably regarding everything dealing with the bodily gestures during prayer [4]. It is also true that, for many believers, putting the Sunna into practice entails, first and foremost, copying what they know about the Prophet's outward behavior in day-to-day life, and to model what they do, what they eat, what they wear, and so forth on what he did. For all this, it is impossible to reduce practices attributed to the Prophet (*ittibāʿ al-nabī*) to easily observable formal demonstrations like these. Conformity to the "Muhammadan model" is also, and perhaps above all, the keystone for all initiatory teaching in Islam.

This is what the short work to be discussed in the coming pages – ʿAbd al-Karīm al-Jīlī's *Qāb qawsayn* – intends to show. Countless texts in Sufi literature deal with *ittibāʿ al-nabī*; besides the fact that it is part of the *umma*'s common heritage and deals with the very birth of Islam, it is also true that the idea of the Prophet as exemplar lies at the heart of Muslim spiritual practice. My attention is drawn to Jīlī's text because it is a remarkable document for a number of reasons. Let us be clear at the outset, however: this in no way means that the teachings the author professes are fundamentally novel; far from it.

"I was sent to perfect noble traits of character" [6], says a hadith meditated upon by generations of Sufis even before the 14th century when Jīlī lived. In their eyes, the prophetic model was seen much more as a way of being than it was a way of life: exemplary in his outward actions, God's Messenger was also an example, *a fortiori*, by his inner life, which reflected his relationship to God and ranked him both as the most perfect servant who ever walked the earth and, consequently, the unsurpassed paradigm of sanctity [7].

It is important to remember that, from the perspective of the Muslim mystical tradition, it is only by fulfilling his role as "God's servant" (*ʿabd*) – which is to be his role for all of eternity – that man is able to actualize the theomorphism conferred upon him, in potentiality, by his original status as *imago Dei*. Consequently, it is also only in this way that man is able to rise to the highest degree of sanctity – that in which he is truly the stainless mirror in which God might contemplate His Names. Palingenesis – in other words, the restoration of the Primordial Man – implies the most radical renunciation of both any will of one's own and any claim to autonomy, to the point of washing away any trace of ego that, in the fallen man, might mask the Divine "I."

Theomorphism thus blossoms in the simplest, most stripped-down obedience to divine prescriptions. With his entire being subjugated to Divine Law – at every instant and regardless of the circumstances – the saint actually takes on the "noble traits of character," which are nothing less than the divine nature with which every man is endowed at the dawn of Creation and of which the Prophet (according to the *tasawwuf* masters) is the full and complete epiphany. "His nature was the Qur'an," as the Prophet's wife A'isha said about him. From this Ibn Arabi concluded that "He who was not alive at the time of the Prophet but wishes to see him should contemplate the Qur'an, for there is no difference between the act of contemplating it, and contemplating God's Messenger. It is as if the Qur'an had taken on a bodily form with the name Muhammad b. Abd Allāh" [8]. In other words, what the Qur'an, God's word, says in its form as the Book, the Prophet represents this in his form as a man; he incarnates the Qur'an in his example, that of the most absolute servitude, by virtue of the fact he is *khayr al-anām*, "the best of creatures."

"FOLLOW ME, GOD WILL LOVE YOU" [9]

The spiritual quest also requires, of necessity, subjugation to the "Muhammadan model" (a conformity implying strict observance to the divine commandments, of course). Modeling one's life on the Prophet is both the point of departure and the final goal of this quest: "Make your love for Me authentic by following My Beloved, for no one will come to Me without first loving him and following his path, for his path is the ideal path; it gives access to the Supreme Beloved" [10].

It is to Abū 'Uthmān al-Hīrī (d. 298/910) that, according to Sulamī, we are indebted for the interpretation of Sura 3, verse 31, positing *ittibā' al-nabī* as foundational for any spiritual quest in Islam: "Say: If you love God, *follow me* (*ittabi'ūnī*); God will love you" [11]. Al-Hīrī, an eminent representative of the Malāmatī movement in Nishapur in the third century of Islam, is here referring to the cardinal principle driving, in Islamic mysticism, any perception of the *itinerarium in Deum*. According to this principle, modeling one's life on the Prophet's actions is the sole route of access to the highest spiritual realization, the route that, from "theomimesis" (*al-takhalluq bi akhlāq Allāh*) leads the spiritual seeker to supreme union, "theosis" (*al-tahaqquq bi akhlāq Allāh*). To be clear, according to the spiritual masters, rare are those who reach this highest degree of sanctity, where discarding the self takes place to the point that the seeker is henceforth "without name or qualities" [12]. And yet it is only at this price that man becomes God's *khalīfa*, properly speaking – His representative in the strictest sense of the term [13]. And even then he does not reach the summit of this spiritual abode: only the Prophet has this privilege. Imam Ja'far al-Sādiq was stressing this point as early as Islam's second century, when his commentary on the above-mentioned verse from Sura 3 said: "God enjoined the conscience of the Just to follow Muhammad so that they might know – regardless of the quality of their excellence or the height of their rank – that *they can neither surpass him nor even equal him*" [14].

What we are being told here is that the Prophet's spiritual status is a singular phenomenon in the course of spiritual history: no being other than him has reached perfection in its most absolute form. He is frequently referred to as *al-insān al-kāmil* (the "Perfect Man") by Muslim spiritual writers, an expression that later entered into the technical lexicon of Sufism [15], even if the notion had been present, embryonically, as early as Islam's second century, according to imam Ja'far.

It should be noted in this regard that although some writers have used *al-insān al-kāmil* in reference to the person who is the "Pole" (*qutb*) – that is, the saint who plays the highest ranking role in the initiatory hierarchy at a certain period in history – the two terms have been transposed, so this is only valid when the individual in question at a specific time is the Prophet's "substitute" (*nā'ib*) – or more precisely, the substitute for the "Muhammadan Spirit" that, according to Ibn Arabī, is at every point in history the only true Pole, the only true center, of the universe.

It was actually the author of the *Futūhāt Makkiya* who finally elaborated a true "Muhammadology," in the sense that all his initiatory teachings, as well as his entire hagiological, prophetological, and soteriological doctrine, fell under the umbrella concept of the "Muhammadan Reality" (*haqīqa muhammadiyya*). This is the preferred expression in the terminology of *tasawwuf* designating the archetypal Muhammadan Entity – which is seen as the Principle for all spiritual life.

Jīlī, as we shall see, was in complete agreement with Ibn Arabī regarding this question of the Prophet's spiritual supremacy and his primordial role in the sphere of sainthood. More importantly, the *Qāb qawsayn* was somewhat of a culminating peak in the Muhammadology that Ibn Arabī elaborated.

Notes

[1] Qur'an 33:21.

[2] MUSLIM, n.d., "*musafirūn*,"139, I, p. 513, gives a different version of this sentence attributed to A'isha, one often connected to verse 68:4: "In truth, you are of a sublime nature" (IBN ARABĪ, 1911, IV, p. 60).

[3] GOLDZIHER, 1984, p. 23

[4] FIERRO, 1987, pp. 69-90.

[5] Islamic scholars often translate *ittibā' al-nabī* by the Latin *imitatio prophetae*, but the expression *sequela prophetae* seems a better fit, in the way that *sequela Christi* does in reference to the famous saying *nudus Christi nudum sequi*. [The American English translator of this work has chosen to render the author's *sequela prophetae* in terms referring to the "daily actions or practices of the Prophet," for an audience, even of scholars, that may be less familiar with Latin than their French-speaking colleagues.]

[6] WENSINCK, 1936-1969, II, p. 75.

[7] On this question, cf. CHODKIEWICZ, 1994 (b).

[8] IBN ARABĪ, 1911, IV, p. 61; this statement should be seen in the context of the event described in the beginning of *ibid.*, I, p. 48, where Ibn Arabī describes his encounter with the *fatā* in which "he reads" the contents of the *Futūhāt*. On this point, cf. CHODKIEWICZ, 2005 (a), pp. 435-461. Cf. also a similar episode where Ibn Arabī mentions his encounter in Fez with the Pole, in whom he "contemplates the secrets" (IBN ARABĪ, 1948 [b], p. 14).

[9] Qur'an, 3:31.

[10] SULAMĪ, 2001, I, p. 96.

[11] This Qur'anic injunction is not unlike what Jesus said, according to Luke (14:26) and Matthew (10:37-38).

[12] IBN ARABĪ, 1911, IV, p. 13.

[13] On this subject, cf. Ibn Arabī's interpretation (*ibid.*, II, p. 563, III, p. 65, IV, pp. 135-136) of verse 42:11, *laysa ka-mithlihi shay'un*; cf. also CHODKIEWICZ, 1994 (a), p. 37.

[14] SULAMĪ, p. 2001, I, p. 95. With a few minor changes, our translation is the same as NWYIA, 1991, p. 183.

[15] HAKĪM, 1981, p. 160, claims that Ibn Arabī was the very first writer to use this expression, although given the fact that a number of authors who preceded him have yet to be studied, we cannot be certain of her claim.

Chapter Six

"At no time is Muhammad absent from any location" [1]

"UNITE ME WITH HIM" [2]

I am indebted to Valerie Hoffman for estimating the contribution that Jīlī's *Qāb qawsayn* brought to the question of devotion to the Prophet, as well as its practical and doctrinal implications. Unless I am mistaken, the American professor was the first to bring to scholars' attention the importance of Jīlī's short work in this regard, which she did during a conference in Berkeley in 1994 [3]. Her presentation, "Annihilation in the Messenger in the Writings of Jīlī," dealt specifically with passages in which Jīlī was looking at what annihilation in the Messenger (*fanāʾ fī l-rasūl*) involved – granted, Jīlī himself did not use the term – and how to achieve it using the practice of *taʿalluq*, attachment to the Prophet. The practice essentially involved assiduous recitation of *tasliya*, "praying on the Prophet." The passages in question, especially those in the second-to-last of the *Qāb qawsayn*'s seven chapters, surely constitute the high point of the Yemeni teacher's Muhammadology, though he also addressed the issue in his *Kamālāt ilāhiyya* ("The Divine Perfections"), a work to which he refers at several points, as we shall see.

It should also be clarified, however, that Professor Hoffman's decision to focus on these passages from *Qāb qawsayn* was due to the fact that the theme of *fanāʾ fī l-rasūl* lay at the heart of a thirty-year (and longer) debate among renowned students of Islam regarding the concept of "neo-Sufism"; it was her opinion that Jīlī's text could shed light on the debate.

It is not my intention to provide a detailed history of this controversy, since it is only incidental to the present work. However, to the extent that I, like Hoffman, am of the opinion that the *Qāb qawsayn* constitutes an essential piece of evidence regarding the *fanā' fī l-rasūl* question, and especially since my research has led to information that had not been available to her – research that supports her point of view – I feel it necessary to review the primary issues.

The prevailing opinion until recently was that the 18th and 19th centuries were characterized by the emergence of new brotherhoods – Sanūsiyya, Khatmiyya, Idrīsiyya, Rashīdiyya, among others – where the common denominator was promoting a Sufism stripped both of themes characteristic of Ibn Arabī's school and of "suspect" popular practices (*samā'*, *ziyārat al-qubūr*, "visiting tombs," and so forth), and characterized by a theoretically totally new Prophetocentrism, as seen in the importance that the founders of these brotherhoods placed on *ittibā' al-nabī* in spiritual life in general, on the one hand, and on *fanā' fī l-rasūl* in the process of spiritual realization, on the other [4].

The primary instigator of this neo-Sufism seemed to be Ahmad Ibn Idrīs (d. 1253/1837) who, they say, wanted to lay the foundations for a vast pan-Islamic movement with a mission to fight the Christian invader. His doctrine would have practitioners follow the "Muhammadan Way" (*al-tarīqa al-muhammadiyya*): in short, emulating Ibn Taymiyya.

This view of things – its origins stemming from the works of F. Rahman, and then supported by John O. Voll and J. S. Trimingham, to name the principal protagonists – was seriously challenged beginning in 1990, notably by the works of R. S. O'Fahey and B. Radtke. The former published a serious monograph devoted to Ahmad Ibn Idrīs [5], in which, supported by the writings of the latter – and not, as had previously been the case, by summaries of these events from authors in the service of colonial empires – a very different picture was painted of the Moroccan master: that of a spiritual guide (*murshid*) who had not even dreamed of founding a brotherhood, let alone a pan-Islamic movement. He limited his activity to *tarbiya*, the "spiritual education" of his followers, with teachings – based, as they should have been, on *ittibā' al-nabī* – bearing the clear markings of Ibn Arabī.

We are indebted to Radtke, in part for a widely regarded article in *Der Islam* in 1994, coauthored by O'Fahey, in which the two scholars dismantled, point by point, the arguments proffered by proponents of the idea of neo-Sufism [6]. But Radtke also authored a series of articles, all exemplary in both erudition and methodology, that led to significant advances in our understanding of 18th century Sufism.

That this Sufism was strongly oriented toward the figure of the Prophet was never in doubt, as Radtke himself agrees [7]. Explicit references to the concept of "Muhammadan Light" (*nūr muhammadī*) in the works of Ibn Idrīs, especially in his *ʿIqd al-nafīs*, are especially deserving of our attention [8]. But *nūr muhammadī*, once again, was in no way a novel idea. As has been noted before, this theme in Islamic doctrine had been gaining momentum as the centuries advanced, to the point of becoming a leitmotif of literature devoted to the "good works of the Prophet." Reading Nabhānī's (d. 1350/1931) *Jawāhir al-bihār* makes this clear: the compendium is less than four volumes long, yet in it the author gathered numerous texts addressing the preeminence of the Prophet. The great majority of these were by later authors – mostly from the 15th to the 19th centuries – and primarily in *tasawwuf* circles. As can be seen, *nūr muhammadī* was not only a ubiquitous theme, it was also one that, over the centuries, had risen to the status of a creed in its own right.

On the more specific topic of Ibn Idrīs and his followers, particularly Muhammad al-Sanūsī (d. 1276/1859), we should look at the decisive influence (as B. Radtke has underscored [9]) that the *Kitāb al-Ibrīz* had on their doctrinal formation. The *Kitāb*, in which Ibn al-Dabbāgh (d. 1132/1719), in language entirely his own, outlined a Muhammadology with *nūr muhammadī* at its epicenter, was widely read. Moreover, the great Moroccan Sufi was the second link in one of the initiatory "chains of transmission" (*silsilas*) that also included Ibn Idrīs. Far from unimportant, this was the chain, through Khadir, that connected him directly to the Prophet [10]. No less decisive in this regard were Ibn Arabī's teachings, whose major doctrinal themes, especially those concerning the cosmic dimension of the Prophet's spiritual magisterium, had long been permeating all of Islamic spirituality [11]. We should also note that Ibn Idrīs's spiritual master, ʿAbd al-Wahhāb al-Tāzī [12], was in close contact with the "Akbarian milieu" of the time, since he was both a disciple of Muhammad al-Hifnī (d. 1181/1767) [13] – himself a disciple of Nāblusī, the eminent representative of the Akbarian school in Ottoman Syria – and, at the same time, a follower of the latter's primary heir, Mahmūd al-Kurdī (d. 1195/1781), a diligent reader of the *Futūhāt Makkiyya* and, per the historian Jabartī

(d. 1240/1826), the author of a commentary (after a vision of Ibn Arabī) on the *Fusus al-hikam* [14].

The fact remains that, for Ibn Idrīs and his spiritual heirs, this prophetocentric concept of sanctity entailed both practical implications and specific rituals, like assiduous recitation of "prayer upon the Prophet" (*tasliya*) in hopes of reaching *fanā' fī l-rasūl* [15]. One item should be clarified here: I have several times used the word "Muhammadology," which by definition refers to the contents of a field of knowledge, or a doctrine. However, it should be understood that, for the spiritual thinkers named above who, to one degree or another, participated in either defining or developing the field, what we are talking about is in no way the product of abstract or highly intellectual speculation. Their driving force was a certainty that the Prophet is "the Perfect Man" (*al-insān al-kāmil*); this idea was part and parcel of their faith in God, in the same way that the second part of the *shāhada* ("and Muhammad is His Messenger") is inseparable from from the first ("there is no god but God"). The idea must of necessity be translated into daily life, via behaviors or practices that were typical of the Prophet, on the one hand, and on the other, via performance of certain devotional practices aimed at creating a "link" (*rābita*) connecting them directly to the Prophet. It is significant in this regard that *salat ʿazīmiyya* – the *tasliya* wording passed on by Ibn Idrīs, which he claimed to have received from the Prophet himself [16] – takes place through the following plea: "Unite me with him [the Prophet] as you unite the spirit and the body, on the outside as well as within, whether I sleep or am awake, and make him the spirit of my being [17], in every way, in this world before the hereafter."

THE "MUHAMMADAN WAY"

"To be united with the Prophet" as the spirit is to the body: when all is said and done, these are the defining words of Ibn Idrīs's spirituality, as well as that of those who subscribe to his teachings, most notably Muhammad al-Sanūsi, who in a well-known passage from *Salsabīl al-muʿīn*, defined what is most characteristic of the *tarīqa muhammadiyya*, the "Muhammadan Way," in the following terms:

> As for the *tarīqa muhammadiyya*, it is the path that draws its name from Muhammad, upon whom be Grace and Peace. The teacher of all teachers, Abū Sālim al-ʿAyyāshī, may God be mer-

ciful to him, stated in this regard: [this Muhammadan Way] is specific in how it is representative of the Prophet, even though all paths lead back to him and benefit from his assistance; it consists in its follower [...] being assiduously devoted to recitation of the *tasliya*, to the point that it takes possession of his heart and the veneration he feels toward him [the Prophet] filters into his conscience to the point where when he hears [the Prophet's] name he begins to tremble, to the point where his heart is dominated by contemplation [of the Prophet], and where he appears to be present to the eyes of internal vision [18]. God at this point gives him an abundance of grace, both inside and out, and leaves power over him to no creature other than the Prophet; he sees him whether he is awake or asleep, and he is able to question him about any subject [19].

There are a number of versions of this text, and references to it, a mark of the attention it has drawn from both Muslim writers and scholars of Islam [20]. Might it be that the ideas it expresses are suggesting something innovative? A look at Jīlī's *Qāb qawsayn* (Jīlī lived in the 14th century) says otherwise – an issue to which we shall return. In fact, Sanūsī himself attributes this definition of the "Muhammadan Way" to shaykh Abū Sālim al-ʿAyyāshī (d. 1090/1679), implying that the idea of a *tarīqa muhammadiyya* owes nothing to Sufism's "reformers" in the 18th century. We might also point out that this text appears word-for-word in the beginning of Murtadā al-Zabīdī's [21] (d. 1205/1790) *ʿIqd al-jawhar*, which makes no reference to ʿAyyāshi or even to Hasan al-ʿUjaymī (d. 1113/1702). Sanūsī mentioned the work at the beginning of the *Salsabīl*, and borrowed from it the long passage regarding the *tarīqa muhammadiyya* [22].

In any case, the author of the statement – as well as Muhammad al-Sanūsī, who transcribed the text – was quite conscious that the "Muhammadan Way" belonged to the ancestral heritage of *tasawwuf*, since in the lines that followed he listed the great names in Egyptian Sufism who practiced this "Muhammadan Way," most notably Ahmad al-Zawwāwī (d. 923/1517) and Nūr al-Dīn al-Shūnī (d. 944/1537). Shaʿrānī (d. 973/1565) spent time with both teachers, and was strongly impressed by the deep devotion each showed for the Prophet, who was so integral to their spiritual lives. Ahmad al-Zawwāwī, he says [23], recited the *tasliya* forty thousand times a day, and told him:

> Our Path consists of assiduous recitation of the *tasliya*, until such time that the Prophet keeps us company in our vigils and we become his Companions [*sahāba*] and we are prepared to question him regarding religious issues and regarding hadiths declared to be weak by our learned individuals knowledgeable in such matters, so that we might work according to his words. As long as that has not come to pass, we are not among those who practice *tasliya* assiduously [24].

Here is one definition that, we might agree, states the essentials of the above-mentioned text from the *Salsabīl*. We might add that it is reminiscent of what Ibn Arabī said on the subject...a few centuries earlier:

> There are saints who have an exchange of words [*hadīth*] with the Prophet in the course of a revelation, who remain in his company in the world of revelation and contemplation, and receive his words from him. They will be gathered together with him, like the Companions, in the most noble of places and the most sublime of states. Such a vision must take place in a waking state. This saint then receives directly from the Prophet, who confirms for him the authenticity of certain hadiths whose transmission has been criticized [25].

Nūr al-Dīn al-Shūnī (d. 944/1537), whom Sha'rānī says recited the *tasliya* forty thousand times a day [26], can be traced back to the beginnings of the Egyptian institution of *laylat al-mahyā*, a "night of vigil" (usually Friday night) during which a group of believers devoted their time to reciting the "Prayer upon the Prophet" [27]. According to Najm al-Dīn al-Ghazzī, Shūnī instituted the practice at Al-Azhar mosque in 897 A.H., and less than a century later it had spread to nearly every part of the Muslim world, most notably to Syria [28]. F. Mayer was nevertheless correct in pointing out how difficult it is to determine the precise origins of the practice in each Muslim country, in the sense that worship of the Prophet was spreading continually from century to century, and showing a diversity of forms depending on the time or place [29]. In the Maghreb, for example, as early as the 15th century, recitation of Jazūlī's (d. 869/1465) *Dalā'il al-khayrāt* gave way to weekly gatherings dedicated to a collective reading of the work and blessings upon the Prophet. On top of that, R. Vimercati Sanseverino's research found that Jazūlī was the first of the Maghreban teachers to institute recitation of *tasliya* as an initiatory practice in its own right [30], founding his path on the practice. Shaʿrānī reported that in Yemen some teachers customarily "transmitted" *tasliya* to their followers – the word he uses in this case, *talqīn*, usually refers to transmission from teacher to follower of a specific *dhikr*, a ritual that is one of the several methods by which initiates are connected to Sufi teachers. These students were required to recite intensely until they were able to "meet" the Prophet and ask him questions while in a wakened state [31].

ON ATTACHMENT TO THE PROPHET

Whatever the case, the concept of *tarīqa muhammadiyya* is attested to well before the 16th century. Ibn Taymiyya (d. 728/1328) himself used the expression in the earliest lines of the letter he addressed to shaykh Muhammad al-Manbijī [32]. His disciple Ibn Qayyim al-Jawziyya (d. 751/1350) is moreover said to be the author, according to Safadī, of a treatise titled *al-Risāla al-halabiyya fī l-tarīqa l-muhammadiyya* [33]. The idea of the "Muhammadan Way" lay at the heart of a mystical treatise from the end of the 13th century – the *Sulūk wa l-sayr ilā Llāh*, by Ahmad al-Wāsitī (d. 711/1311) – a treatise that Éric Geoffroy discussed in a rich and detailed study [34]. The son of a Rifāʿī shaykh, and later affiliated with Shādhiliyya, al-Wāsitī ended up joining the small circle of Ibn Taymiyya's (d. 728/1328) disciples, and professing boundless admiration for the him. Al-Wāsitī is thus hard to pin down; in contrast to his teacher, he rejected what Ibn Arabī said about "the oneness of being" (*wahdat al-wujūd*) [35] and denounced certain practices instituted in the brotherhoods, yet he had no hesitation about citing Tirmīdhī's *Khatm al-awliyāʾ* or defending *tasawwuf* against its detractors, if the need arose. This ambivalence permeated his thought about the chain of initiatory transmission, where a dual heritage shows through: that which came via his own initiation into Sufism during his youth, and that transmitted by Ibn Taymiyya who, let us remember, was a member of the Qādiriyya order [36].

The fact remains that some of the principles foundational to his thinking about the "Muhammadan Way" are not completely dissimilar to those underlying the doctrine of *fanāʾ fī l-rāsul*, as it was developed by Ibn Idrīs and his followers. The author of the *Sulūk* did not restrict himself to advocating strict conformity to the prophetic model. This conformity should be both internal and external [37], he stressed, while also recommending that the novice "attach" himself (*taʿalluq*) to the Messenger [38] until such time that he could visualize this presence which would "then accompany [him] for the duration of his initiatory journey" [39].

Let it be remembered that the word *taʿalluq*, which he used numerous times [40] in reference to this manner of attachment to the Prophet, is the same word that Jīlī used (as we shall see) in a similar context in his *Qāb qawsayn*. Not only that, it is also the word that a much later writer, Muhammad al-Sammān (d. 1189/1775) would use in a little work titled *al-Futūhāt al-ilāhiyya fī l-tawajjuhāt al-rūhiyya li l-hadra al-muhammadiyya*. B. Radtke highlighted the importance of this work [41], since it dealt precisely with the spread of the idea of the "Muhammadan Way," and did so at the same time that calling it the *tarīqa muhammadiyya*, properly speaking, was being transmitted widely after Muhammad Birgilī (d. 981/1573) entered the scene [42]. That was actually the title of the somewhat famous treatise in which Birgilī decried the countless "blameworthy innovations" that Sufis had introduced into religious practices throughout the ages. These innovations corrupted the original Islam, which can only be brought back via return to strict practice of the Sunna, here seen exclusively in its most formal form [43]. Birgilī's work found a certain amount of favor in the Ottoman world, and was especially inspirational in the virulent anti-Sufi current known as the Qādīzādelis, popular for a time in Istanbul but also in Cairo and Damascus [44]. The work also gave rise to a number of glosses, for the purpose either of supporting Birgilī's views – as was the case for a work that became the first book printed in both Istanbul (1803) and Bulaq (1825) [45] – or, on the contrary, of challenging them. Most notable among the latter was a treatise by Nābulusī, of course refuting Birgilī's formalist conception of the "Muhammadan Way" [46].

Whatever might be the case, in addition to our seeing the expression in Wāsitī's *Sulūk*, *tarīqa muhammadiyya* also appears in the writing of shaykh Ibn Maymūn al-Fāsī [47] (d. 917/1511) and apparently also that of his follower Ibn ʿArrāq, to whom a treatise on the Muhammadan Way's legal principles is attributed [48]. The term also recurs frequently in the *Mughlī al-huzn*, by shaykh ʿAlwān (d. 936/1530) [49]. It is probable that broader research will discover further mentions of the term in authors before the 16th century [50].

The fact nevertheless remains that Sammān's treatise holds a meaningful place, not because of its development of the concept of *tarīqa muhammadiyya*, but rather due to its extensive propagation in the 18th century. A follower of the three main representatives of Ibn Arabī's school in the Ottoman period – Mustafā al-Bakrī (d. 1162/1749), Muhammad al-Hifnī, and Mahmūd al-Kurdī – Sammān founded the brotherhood that bears his name [51], the Sammāniyya Order, a branch of the Khalwatiyya. One notable member of the order was Ibn Sūda (d. 1209/1795), a well-known intellectual from Fez [52] who also frequently spent time, during a trip to the Middle East, with the famous hadith scholar and lexicographer Murtadā al-Zabīdī (d. 1205/1790) [53]. Al-Zabīdī was one of the individuals responsible for passing down the *khirqa akbariyya*, the initiatory investiture characteristic of Ibn Arabī's spiritual lineage [54]. Ibn Sūda also spent time with Mahmūd al-Kurdī, through whom he became part of an initiatory chain that began with Ibn Arabī [55]. After his return to Morocco, Ibn Sūda taught hadith at the Moroccan university Al-Qarawiyyīn in Fez, and in this role taught both Ibn Idrīs [56] – before Ibn Idrīs left Morocco definitively – and Ibn Kīrān (d. 1227/1812) who, in turn, would later teach hadith to Muhammad Sanūsī [57]. Like Ibn Sudā, Ibn Kirān gained a certain renown in his time as a scholar of hadith, which was thus the subject of the majority of his works with the exception of two: a commentary on Ibn ʿAtāʾ Allāh's *Hikam*, and another dealing with *salāt mashīshiyya* - Ibn Mashīsh's own wording of the *tasliya*, which engendered countless commentaries of its own over the ensuing centuries [58]. Published several years ago in Abu Dhabi [59], the commentary on *salāt mashīshiyya* is permeated by Ibn Arabī's teachings from beginning to end, especially regarding the "Muhammadan Reality."

This leads us to Sammān's *Tawajjuhāt al-rūhiyya*, a short, three-chapter work of only seven folios [60]. The first of the chapters – the densest, by far – addresses the question of "attachment" (*taʿalluq*) to the Prophet in detail. Sammān distinguishes between two complementary types of attachment: "formal" attachment (*sūrī*), consisting of complete and entire conformity to the prophetic model, and "subtle" attachment (*maʿnawī*), which has two stages. In the first, the novice is invited to visualize the Prophet in his bodily form, while keeping Muhammad's unsurpassable perfection so present in his mind that he is able to "dissolve into the Muhammadan Light" [61]; at this point a long description of the concept of the "Muhammadan Reality" ensues. In the second chapter, the writer discusses some of his own visionary experiences, while in the third and last of the chapters he goes back to the theme of the sublime perfection of the Prophet, as it is seen through his physical appearance, his acts, and his words.

As Radtke has justly remarked [62], at the heart of the work is the idea of *tarīqa muhammadiyya*. It was Sammān's intention to outline the methods that allow *suhba* (companionship with the Prophet) to be fully realized, to the point where the Prophet could be communicated with at any moment [63]. We thus find ourselves in the presence of particularly elaborate (albeit uncoordinated) reflections on the "Muhammadan Way." The text is an innovative one, to say the least...though it would not be fair to call Sammān its actual author: of the treatise's three chapters, only the second – an autobiographical chapter, and an extremely short one, at that – can be attributed to him. All the rest, *to the letter*, is borrowed from Jīlī's *Qāb qawsayn*, especially his sixth and seventh chapters, the ones that specifically attracted Valerie Hoffman's attention.

At the end of the paper she presented, Hoffman remarked that she had no evidence to suggest that Jīlī's *Qāb qawsayn* was sufficiently widespread to link it to the main teachers of Sufism in the 18th century [64]. Muhammad al-Sammān's treatise – in reproducing, though without ever saying as much, the *Qāb qawsayn*'s most important passages on methods of attachment to the Prophet – shows that such a connection did exist. It might also be considered relevant that Muhammād al-Sammān was born and raised in Medina. Nabhānī, in his *Jawāhir al-bihār*, stated that one of the three *Qāb qawsayn* manuscripts in his possession had come from the Medina library [65].

One other case of borrowing from the *Qāb qawsayn* has been noted, this time in Ibn Idrīs's circle. In a short work on the wording of prayers appropriate for recitation at the Prophet's gravesite [66], ʿUthmān Mīrghanī (d. 1268/1852) – the youngest of Ibn Idrīs's followers and the founder of the Khatmiyya order – cited, via an abbreviated version of it, the famous *Qāb qawsayn* passage about the two kinds of attachment to the Prophet. In contrast to Sammān, however, he attributed its origin to Jīlī and referred to the *Nāmūs* (a huge work to be dealt with shortly, containing the text of the *Qāb qawsayn*) in the text immediately following the passage.

And finally, let it be added that Radtke noted the existence of an unedited treatise by Ismāʿīl al-Nawwāb dealing with "orientation" (*al-tawajjuh*) and "attachment" (*taʿalluq*) – two key words in both the *Qāb qawsayn* and Sammān's *Tawajjuhāt* – to the Prophet [67]. Perusal of one of these manuscripts [68] shows it to be essentially a collection of passages on the theme of the meta-historical nature of the Prophet's spiritual magisterium, on the one hand, and on the practice of reciting the *tasliya* on the other, with *tasliya* being seen as a ritual practice for inducing a direct and immediate relationship with God's Messenger. Two items are thus recopied: a treatise with a title solemnly proclaiming that "At no time is Muhammad absent from any location" [69], and Sammān's *Tawajjuhāt rūhiyya*, which the author curiously attributes to Mustafā al-Bakrī [70]. Since Ismāʿīl al-Nawwāb was the disciple of Ismāʿīl Rashīd, who was himself a follower of Ibn Idrīs, we see one additional link in the spread of the *Qāb qawsayn* in the 18th and 19th centuries, and of the teachings it brought into Sufi orders from the spiritual heritage of this "Enigmatic Saint" [71].

Notes

[1] Title of a short work copied by NABHĀNĪ, 1998, II, pp. 143-159, though its author's name is not yet known (see below, p. 93).

[2] NABHĀNĪ, 1996 (a), p. 91.

[3] A meeting organized the the Ibn Arabī Society at the University of California at Berkeley, November 1994. A revised version of this paper was published in the *International Journal of Middle East Studies, 31*, 3, 2001.

[4] For a detailed summary of the concept of neo-Sufism and its supporting arguments, cf. O'FAHEY & RADTKE, 1993, and RADTKE, 2005; cf. also the list of debates offered by CHIH & MAYEUR-JAOUEN, 2010, pp. 13-19.

[5] O'FAHEY, 1990.

[6] ID., & RADTKE, 1993; but O'Fahey later qualified his opinion (cf. O'FAHEY, 1997; RADTKE, 2005, p. 293).

[7] ID., 1996 (b), p. 360.

[8] ʿIqd al-nafīs, in NABHĀNĪ, 1998, III, pp. 62-64; cf. also THOMASSEN & RADTKE, 1993, p. 18.

[9] RADTKE, 1996 (b), pp. 331, 355-356; ID., 1996 (a), p. 117; cf. also HOFFMAN, 1999, pp. 358-361.

[10] O'FAHEY & RADTKE, 1993, p. 69; RADTKE, O'FAHEY, & O'KANE, 1996, p. 151; THOMASSEN & RADTKE, 1993, p. 64.

[11] CHODKIEWICZ, 2005 (b).

[12] On Tāzī, cf. O'FAHEY, 1990, pp. 39-44.

[13] CHIH, 2000, pp. 137-149.

[14] Cf. the long note that Jabartī, who was one of his followers, wrote about him (JABARTĪ, 1998, II, pp. 88-96).

[15] THOMASSEN & RADTKE, 1993, pp. 128-131, 148-149.
[16] The Arabic text of this *tasliya* is in NABHANĪ, 1996 (a), p. 91. For translations, cf. PADWICK, 1961, p. 151; O'FAHEY, 1990, pp. 194-195; and RADTKE, O'FAHEY, & O'KANE, 1996, p. 162, for Ibn Idrīs's account of the circumstances under which he heard these words from the Prophet.
[17] "*Rūhan li-dhātī.*" On the meaning of the word *dhāt* here, cf. Radtke's remarks on the use of *dhāt* in the *k. al-Ibrīz* (RADTKE, 1996 [b], p. 350; ID., 1996 [a], pp. 119-121).
[18] SANŪSĪ, 1968 (b), p. 7. The text says *timthāl*, a Qurʾanic term used in the plural in 21:52, with a negative connotation because at issue is the "statues" idolized by Abraham's people. But the text in ZABĪDĪ (ms. [a], folio 74) says *mutammathilan*, which can also be connected to a passage where it has a positive connotation, since in this case it occurs in the verse telling of the angel Gabriel's appearance at the time of the Annunciation (Qurʾan 19:17). I have used it with this second reading of the word in mind.
[19] SANŪSĪ, 1968 (b), p. 7; ZABĪDĪ, ms. (a), folio 74; ʿAYYĀSHĪ, 2006, II, p. 297.
[20] There is a slightly different version of this passage in SANŪSĪ, 1968 (a), p. 49; it was eruditely annotated in RADTKE, 1992, pp. 74-75. Cf. also ID., 1996 (b), pp. 355-356; PADWICK, 1961, pp. 150-151; SCHIMMEL, 1984, p. 226.
[21] ZABIDĪ, ms. (a), folio 74.
[22] GRIL, 2010, p. 74; REICHMUTH, 2010, p. 396.
[23] SHAʿRĀNĪ, 1993, p. 284.
[24] *Ibid.*
[25] IBN ARABĪ, 1911, III, p. 50. We are using the translation by GRIL, 2005, p. 133.
[26] SHAʿRĀNĪ, 1993, p. 284.
[27] ID., n.d., 2nd part, pp. 171-172; *EI2*, "*Mahyā*"; GEOFFROY, 1995 (a), pp. 95, 103.
[28] GHAZZĪ, 1997, II, pp. 214ff.
[29] MEIER, 1999 (b), pp. 671-672.
[30] VIMERCATI SANSEVERINO, 2012, pp. 336-337.
[31] SHAʿRĀNĪ, 1985, 1st part, p. 32.
[32] IBN TAYMIYYA, n.d., I, 1st part, p. 161.
[33] SAFADĪ, 1998, IV, p. 370; HAJJĪ KHALĪFA, n.d., I, p. 871.
[34] GEOFFROY, 1995 (b).
[35] He was the author of a short epistle condemning the teachings of the *Fusūs al-hikam* (YAHIA, 1964, I, p. 114)
[36] GEOFFROY, 1995 (b), note 91.
[37] *Ibid.*, p. 90.
[38] *Ibid.*, p. 89.
[39] *Ibid.*, p. 90.
[40] WĀSITĪ, ms., folios 58b, 59a, 96a, 97b, etc.
[41] RADTKE, 1996 (b), p. 355.
[42] *Ibid.* CORNELL, 1992, p. 203, is of the opinion that the first to outline the concept of the "Muhammadan Way" was shaykh Jazūlī ʿAbd Allāh al-Ghazwānī (d. 935/1528).
[43] SCHLEGELL, 1977, pp. 85-95.
[44] *Ibid.*, pp. 80-85.

[45] SEDGWICK, 2005, p. 34.
[46] SCHLEGELL, 1977, pp. 88-95; PAGANI, 2010.
[47] GEOFFROY, 2008, p. 141.
[48] BAGHDĀDĪ, 1951, II, col. 232, indicates the title as being *al-Qawā'id al-shar'iyya li sāliki al-tarīqa al-muhammadiyya.* GHAZZI (1997, I, p. 65) nevertheless attributes a *Risāla ilā man intasaba ilā l-tarīqa al-muhammadiyya* to him.
[49] GEOFFROY, 1995 (a), p. 270, note 3.
[50] JĪLĪ, 2004, p. 13, uses the expression *tarīq muhammadī.*
[51] Cf. *Arabic Literature of Africa,* ch. V; DREWES, 1992; GABORIEAU & GRANDIN, 1996, p. 72.
[52] VIMERCATI SANSEVERINO, 2012, p. 490.
[53] REICHMUTH, 2009, p. 187.
[54] ADDAS, 1989, p. 371.
[55] HAWWĀT, 1994, II, p. 683.
[56] O'FAHEY, 1990, p. 35.
[57] *Ibid.,* pp. 36-37; ID. & RADTKE, 1993, p. 66. On Ibn Kīrān, cf. ZIRIKLĪ, 1984, VI, p. 178.
[58] A number of these commentaries are retranscribed, most notably the one by 'Abd Allāh Mīrghanī al-Mahjūb (d. 1207/1793), in NABHĀNĪ, 1998, II, pp. 519-531.
[59] IBN KĪRĀN, 1999. On tension between Ibn Kīrān and Ahmad Tijānī, cf. EL ADNANI, 2005, pp. 46-47.
[60] This concerns SAMMĀN, ms., folios 53-59.
[61] *Ibid.,* folio 56.
[62] RADTKE, 1966 (b), p. 332.
[63] SAMMĀN, ms., folio 55b.
[64] HOFFMAN, 1999, p. 358.
[65] NABHĀNĪ, 1998, IV, p. 259.
[66] This concerns the *Bāb al-fayd wa l-madad min hadrat al-rasūl* (cf. *Arabic Literature of Africa,* p. 189, num. 4); the text in question is reproduced in NABHĀNĪ, 1983, I, p. 366.
[67] NAWWĀB, ms., folios 1-49 (cf. O'FAHEY & RADTKE, 1993, p. 71, note 72; *Arabic Literature of Africa,* p. 157, num. 2). On al-Nawwāb, cf. SEDGWICK, 2005, pp. 89-91.
[68] The ms. in question is by NAWWĀB, folios 1-49 (may be found on the Internet at http://makhtota.ksu.edu.sa).
[69] *Ta'rīf ahl al-islām wa l-īmān bi anna Muhammad lā yakhlū minhu makān wa lā zamān,* in *ibid.,* folios 13-25; is was also reproduced in NABHĀNĪ, 1998, II, pp. 143-159, who attributed it to Nūr al-Dīn Halabī (d. 1044/1635), who could not have known shaykh al-Shūnī (d. 944/1537), though the author of the treatise claims on several occasions that al-Shūnī was his teacher.
[70] NAWWĀB, ms., folio 28.
[71] We might note that "Enigmatic Saint" was the main title of the monograph O'Fahey devoted to Ibn Idrīs (O'FAHEY, 1990).

Chapter Seven

"At a distance of two bows or closer" [1]

Did ʿAbd al-Karīm al-Jīlī really exist? That might be a fair question, were it not for works that bear his name and their influence on *tasawwuf* literature. His Arab historian contemporaries left no record of his ever having set foot on the earth, with the exception of a fleeting note by Ibn al-Ahdal [2], an adversary, if there ever was one, of Ibn Arabī's school. Nor is there a single word about him in *tabaqāt* works (biographical dictionaries of all kinds), not even in Sharjī's (d. 983/1488) [3] *Tabaqāt al-khawwās*, despite the fact that its focus was on pious individuals who had lived in Yemen, and Sharjī's happened to be a work containing information about Zabīd Sufis that Jīlī associated with. Until recently, this puzzling absence is largely responsible for much of the uncertainty surrounding both Jīlī's place of birth and the date of his death. Thanks to the research of Ridha Atlagh [4], light has been cast on both of these details. According to what Jīlī himself said in a poem [5], he made his entrance in India, in Calcutta, on the first day of *muharram* 767 (18 September, 1365). He also said that his father took him to Aden, where he passed away while his son was still an adolescent. The same document also contains a detail from one of Jīlī's sons, saying that he died in Zabīd on Saturday, 28 *jumāda II*, 811 (January, 1409).

Only forty-three years of age when he passed away, Jīlī appears to have left no disciples, and no *tarīqa* to perpetuate his memory. He continued to live on only through his writings, which here and there dropped autobiographical breadcrumbs allowing us to follow a few of the major stops along his terrestrial and spiritual itinerary [6]. We thus know that in 790 he was living in India [7], and that six years later he was in Zabīd where he had two visions of the Prophet, one of which described him as appearing dressed in the seven entitative attributes of divinity [8]. In 799 he was in Mecca [9], returning to Zabīd the next year, where in a second visionary episode he met all the prophets and saints [10]. Two years after that, in 802, he made the pilgrimage and, during a time of recollection at the Prophet's tomb, had another vision concerning Muhammad's "sublime nature" (*khuluq ʿazīm*) [11]. The next year, in 803, he went to Damascus, and it was there, he tells us, that he gained access to the "station of servitude" (*maqām al-ʿubūda*) [12]. In the following month he was in Gaza [13], during which time he began work on the *Kamālāt ilāhiyya fī l-sifāt al-muhammadiyya* ("The Divine Perfections in the Attributes of the Prophet") – a work where his beliefs about everything related to the Prophet were fully laid out – after which he went on to Cairo [14]. In 805, he was finally back in Zabīd, where he finished his work on the *Kamālāt ilāhiyya* [15].

One thing is certain: Jīlī traveled frequently, at least some of which was for professional reasons; a passage in his *Haqīqat al-haqā'iq* says that he was a merchant before turning full-time to the mystical life [16]. It is also certain that Zabīd, an intellectual haven in Rasulid Yemen, was his home base, and that it was there that his spiritual teacher, Ismāʿīl al-Jabartī (d. 806/1403), lived [17].

An eminent representative of Yemeni Sufism during Rasulid times, Jabartī is remembered as a fervent partisan of Ibn Arabī. His name appears in one of the "chains of transmission" (*silsila*) in a collection of prayers attributed to Ibn Arabī, as it does in several of the chains relating to the *Futūhāt* [18] and, even more importantly, in one of the lineages in the *khirqa akbariyya* [19]. Beyond all this, Jabartī was not content just to study Ibn Arabī by himself: the Shaykh al-Akbar was required reading for everyone around him. Ibn Hajar al-ʿAsqalānī (d. 852/1449), who met him, claimed that he turned away any students who did not have a copy of the *Fusūs* [20]. This particular testimony was corroborated by Jīlī, who told a story in his *Marātib al-wujūd* that reveals the importance – for those wishing to make spiritual progress – that Jabartī placed on the study of Ibn Arabī's works [21]. It goes without saying that Jabartī's proselytism for Ibn Arabī was an irritation for the Yemeni ulama, who were equally critical of the frequent "spiritual concert" (*samāʿ*) sessions he organized in his *zawiya*; Khazrajī (d. 812/1409) claimed that one of his disciples went into ecstasy in one of these sessions...and died [22]. But Jabartī was under the protection of the sovereign, al-Ashraf (778-803/1377-1401) [23], who, like several of both his predecessors and his successors [24] was very much a supporter of the Sufis, and especially of Jabartī, who was a close confidant [25].

The support that most of the Rasulid sovereigns – they were successors to the Ayyūbids, and like them, defenders of Sunni Islam – showered upon the Sufis is partially explained by the political situation at the time: as they occupied only part of Yemen, basically the southern region, they were in armed conflict with the Zaydīs, and in great need of local support. A number of them – most notably al-Muzaffar (647-694/1249-1295) [26], al-Ashraf, and his successor al-Nāsir (803-827/1401-1424) [27] – were similarly driven by spiritual aspirations and underwrote the construction of a number of mosques and madrasas. In 790, al-Ashraf took the initiative to organize a sizable "spiritual concert" on the coast, to which all the Sufi masters of the region were invited [28]. It was also al-Ashraf who, in 796, invited Fīrūzābādī (d. 817/1415) – a famous hadith scholar and lexicologist – to his court, giving him one of his daughters in marriage, and naming him "qadi general" of Yemen [29]. Whence the resentment of the ulama, who launched a defamation campaign against Fīrūzābādī criticizing especially his frequent references to Ibn Arabī. This led to Fīrūzābādī's reply via a fatwa that later became famous: he praised Ibn Arabī [30]. When al-Ashraf died, his son Nāsir named qadi Ibn al-Raddād, one of Jabartī's closest disciples, to this same post. Ibn al-Raddād, like his teacher, was a diligent reader of Ibn Arabi [31].

Jīlī's work thus comes from an environment singularly favorable to *tasawwuf* and the study of Ibn Arabī's teachings. Because his writings have largely been unpublished, and thus little researched, he remained almost unknown. In fact, no one really knows exactly how much Jīlī actually wrote, as a number of his writings are no longer extant. Here is what we do know: Ridha Atlagh's inventory lists eleven titles [32] of extant manuscripts that Jīlī certainly authored. Two of those works are large compendiums containing a number of treatises: the *Haqīqat al-haqā'iq*, which Jīlī says has thirty parts, though only three of these are currently known; and *Nāmūs al-a'zam*, containing forty treatises of which we currently have seven, one of which is his *Qāb qawsayn* [33]. The three works just cited have been examined by only a small number of scholars, and their spread into the Sufi world was limited – though meaningful, at least in the case of the *Qāb qawsayn*.

Things were very different regarding the widely read and appreciated *Insān kāmil*, as is indicated by the multitude of copies that circulated throughout the entire Muslim world, as well as by the number of editions of the work that were done, the first of which dates back to 1293 A.H. [34]. There is no doubt about the fact that this was the work responsible both for Jīlī being known to later generations and for his being known as one of the major representatives of Ibn Arabī's school. Titus Burckhardt, we should remember, published a partial translation of the work for the first time in 1953 [35].

But there is another side to this coin. It was essentially on *Insān kāmil* that Muslim writers and scholars of Islam based their appreciation of Jīlī's teachings. But just as Ibn Arabī's *Fusūs al-hikam* (the work that was the focus of his adversaries' attacks) was far from representative of all aspects of his metaphysical and hagiological teachings, Jīlī's *Insān kāmil*, which synthesized his metaphysics and prophetology, says not a word about ideas that he developed elsewhere. The work is similarly paradoxical in the way that – while its author is both flagrant and frequent in recognizing his debt to Ibn Arabī – it is also here that, three times and with considerable severity, Jīlī calls his authority into question [36]. As Chodkiewicz has shown [37], however, the importance of Jīlī's criticism of Ibn Arabī should not be overestimated, in the sense that it focused on only one issue specifically and this was largely due to Jīlī's misunderstanding of some of Ibn Arabī's doctrinal statements (the wording of which can lead to confusion). As a matter of fact, Jīlī was not alone among Ibn Arabī's interpreters in expressing reserve about one aspect of his teaching or another [38] that clearly troubled them. There were a number of others who skipped silently, and deliberately, over some of his ideas, especially in regard to his universalist idea of divine mercy.

The fact remains that the author of *Insān kāmil* sticks fully to the foundational theses of Ibn Arabī's teachings, both those related to metaphysics and those dealing with hagiology and prophetology. His adherence is actually not limited to the intellectual: Jīlī, like the author of the *Futūhāt* "speaks only of what he tastes" [39], only of what his own spiritual experience allowed him to know. Whence, precisely, the difference in accent between the two bodies of work, that of the Shaykh al-Akbar and that of his heir, Jīlī. But here and there, points of view (in the proper sense of the term) do diverge: from the peaks where their respective spiritual ascensions led them, the landscape below certainly would have its similarities, but it would not look exactly the same.

"PLACE THE PROPHET BEFORE YOU" [40]

In other words, Jīlī wrote as a witness, not as a theoretician. This is particularly true regarding everything in his writing related to "Muhammadology," the principles of which he drew from his spiritual experience, and more specifically from the two visions of the Prophet referred to earlier, which evidently both marked him deeply and gave shape to his teachings on the subject.

The first vision took place in Zabīd in 796 [41] – Jīlī was thus not yet thirty – and came upon him during a spiritual concert organized by his teacher, al-Jabartī, during which one of the participants was chanting verse 87 from Sura al-Hijr: "We have granted you the seven often-repeated verses and the sublime Qur'an" [42]:

> God, to Him be glory, then had me see His Prophet with the seven entitative attributes. That is: life, knowledge, will, power, hearing, sight, and speech: then I saw him, upon him be Grace and Peace, after he had clothed himself with His Attributes, as *the very essence of the Invisible* [ayn dhāt al-ghā'ib] in the ipseity of the world of mysteries, and it is to this that the end of the verse "and the sublime Qur'an" refers.

The experience of this vision thus allowed Jīlī to realize fully the "sublime nature" [43] of the Prophet, in that he – via his ontological status, nuskhat al-haqq – is the "image of God" and he consequently possesses all the divine attributes [44]. There is nothing novel about this idea in itself; it is actually part of the doctrinal concept regarding the insuperable perfection of the Prophet which, as we have seen, was taking shape as early as Imam Ja'far's time [45]. Nor was Jīlī the first to propose such an exegesis of verse 87 of Sura 15. Although admittedly it is concisely worded, we find such an exegesis in a treatise attributed to Ibn Arabī, but actually written by Muhammad Wafā (d. 765/1363), the Egyptian master whose teachings were largely inspired by the Shaykh al-Akbar (whom the author never referred to by name) [46].

Though I have not encountered an analogous interpretation in any of Ibn Arabī's writings directly relating to the verse in question, it goes without saying that he shared this point of view: the

Prophet, being the flesh and blood manifestation of the "Muhammadan Reality" – which, he says somewhat allusively in a passage from the *'Anqā'* [47], is God's *mithl*, His "equal" referred to in verse 42:11 (*Laysa kamithlihi shay'un*) – he necessarily takes on all the divine attributes [48]. Ibn Arabī nevertheless stops short of comparing the Prophet's essence to God's, as Jīlī does both in this text and elsewhere. It should be underscored that Ibn Arabī is always careful to express himself elliptically, and allusively, when addressing this topic. This can be seen in the above-mentioned *'Anqā'* passage, as well as in other texts where he addresses the issue of the Prophet's essential nature [49]. To the best of my knowledge, he never formally identified the Prophet's essence as being God's.

Understandably, Jīlī never worried about oratorical precautions. Such was particularly the case in *Kamālāt ilāhiyya*, where he made statements that, surprisingly, did not get him taken off to be burned at the stake [50]. Thus, he finished the *khutba* in this work with the following surprising profession of faith: "I attest that there is no God but God, the Lord of Muhammad and his essential reality [*ḥaqīqatuhu*]" [51]. Elsewhere he does not hesitate to declare: "The knowledge that the Prophet has of God is the same knowledge that God has of Himself" [52]. And again, "God is the reality of his essence, and His attributes are his attributes" [53]. No less surprising is his assertion that "the Qur'an is his [the Prophet's] word" [54], which, by the way, led him to a surprising "slip of the pen" [55].

There is thus a quite clear difference in emphasis between Ibn Arabī's texts and Jīlī's, apparently due to two factors. The first is the fact that the author of the *Futūḥāt* places tremendous importance on observance of the rules of *adab* - the rules customarily observed when giving oneself permission to debate topics dealing with religion, but which Ibn Arabī himself refrains from respecting when expressing his ideas – for he wants to hold as closely as possible to "divine expression" such as it is understood from the Qur'an and the Hadith [56]. This concern for molding his language as much as possible on that of the Divine Word not only leads to word choice, but in some cases also to moments of silence, or at least to evasive or ambiguous phrasing, and even to poetic language. When dealing with "Muhammadan Reality," then, he is quick to debate its nature or its mode of being - and he consequently refrains from wording as explicit as what we see in Jīlī's works – but focuses more on defining its cosmic and transhistorical role, doing so with the support of two scriptural arguments: the hadith "I was a prophet when Adam was still between water and clay" and the Qur'anic verse, "And We have sent you to all of humanity" [57], a literal reading of which allowed him to make his point legitimately while expressing himself, in this case, without the slightest ambiguity. Let me stress, however, that Ibn Arabī never referred to any of the many hadiths used by others regarding the theme of *nūr muhammadī:* not the famous hadith reported by Jābir b. ʿAbd Allāh ("The first thing that God created was the light of your Prophet..."), and not any of the traditions that, in one way or another, announced "Were it not for you, I would not have created the universe" (*law lāka...*) [58].

These traditions abound in Jīlī's writings, on the other hand, where not the least concern is expressed regarding their validity [59]. Jīlī probably did not benefit from the same quality of hadith education as Ibn Arabī did; the "science of hadith" (ʿilm al-hadīth) was held in particularly high esteem in Andalusia during the Shaykh al-Akbar's time and, we should also remember, he considered the field to be of such a sacred nature that he spent his entire life studying it [60]. In any case, we see a number of traditions in Jīlī's writings whose authenticity is suspect, to say the least. Such is the case for two other hadiths mentioned above, where the cosmic role of the Prophet is at issue. According to the first, Muhammad is supposed to have said: "I proceed from God and the believers proceed from me" (*anā min Allāh wa l-muʾminūn minnī*) [61], a tradition that Jīlī cites a number of times, particularly in the *Kamālāt ilāhiyya,* the *Qāb qawsayn,* and *al-Kahf wa l-raqīm* – three works focusing entirely on the theme of the Prophet's preeminence [62]. He uses it to establish via scriptural sources that the Prophet is the isthmus linking the universe to God. The second hadith appears in *al-Kahf wa l-raqīm* as follows [63]: "There is no thorn that pricks the foot of any of us without me feeling the pain" [64]. The underlying idea here being, as we see, that the Prophet is connected to each of the believers individually [65].

However, the principal reason for the discrepancy between Ibn Arabī's writings and those of Jīlī on this issue is to be sought in the birth of the *Kamālāt ilāhiyya,* and it is here that we see the most audacious of the latter's statements relating to the Prophet's "sublime nature." The source of the work was actually a vision that occurred in Medina on 24 *dhū l-qaʿda* 802 (October, 1400) – thus just after Jīlī had finished the pilgrimage rites. He tells about it as follows [66]:

> On 24 *dhū l-qaʿda* 802, I was given a vision of the Prophet, in Medina, in the *rawda* [67]. I saw him, may Grace and Peace be upon him, on the supreme horizon [*al ufuq al-aʿlā*] [68] and the border [*al-mustawā*] of the sublime, there where there is no "where," like a pure, absolute essence actualizing what is divine in a perfect and total manner. I heard someone located to his right chant the verse: "Say: He, God, is One" [69] and who, while pronouncing "He, God" was showing [me] the Muhammadan receptacle, and I repeated the same thing. When I returned to the world of creatures, I saw this same Sura inscribed on one of the window panels facing his tomb, though I had not noticed it before; and the Sura is still written there today. I then realized that he who had transcribed it at that place had done so after having contemplated the epiphany of Muhammadan Reality during sublime contemplation.

This vision of the Prophet thus confirms and complements the vision that had occured in Zabīd a few years earlier. The clearly worded correlation between the first words of the first verse of Sura 112, "He, God," and the epiphany of the Muhammadan Presence radically intensifies the impact of the visionary experience, completely explaining the title of the work that proceeds from it: "The Divine Perfections in Muhammadan Attributes" (*al-Kamālāt al-ilāhiyya fī l-sifāt al-muhammadiyya*). Jīlī began writing the work barely three months after the event, 1 *rabīʿ awwal* 803 [70], the month during which the Prophet's *mawlid* ("birth") is celebrated. It was moreover by divine injunction that he decided to set in writing the knowledge and certitudes he had drawn from the visionary episode [71], and which the third chapter, especially, echoes: using as a basis the verse declaring "In truth, you are of a sublime nature" [72] – which (like so many others before him) he related to Aʾisha's famous statement "His nature was the Qurʾan" – Jīlī was attempting to show that all the Names of God, without exception, apply to the Prophet, who actualized them "on the formal plane and on the sublime plane, both outside and inside [...]" [73].

This being the case, Jīlī's Muhammadology cannot be boiled down to the few pithy phrases I have cited here. As is the case for

Ibn Arabī, to whom Jīlī was indebted, the latter's ideas unfold on two different planes; one is meta-historical, and governed by the idea of the "Muhammadan Reality," while the second is initiatory, and oriented around the idea of *ittibāʿ al-nabī*.

For the first of these, Jīlī uses key ideas from Ibn Arabī's teachings: particularly, the both cosmic and trans-historical dimensions of the spiritual magisterium exercised by the Prophet who, due to his ontological preeminence, holds this position for all eternity. The Prophet is thus on the one hand the spiritual father of all prophets – who are actually "substitutes" (*nawwāb*) for the "Muhammadan Reality" sent toward men – and on the other, the one saint from whom, among all the saints without exception and regardless of their respective confessions, they inherit that which qualifies them to be saints (knowledge, charismata, states, stations, and so forth): "characteristics" they draw from the tabernacle of the Muhammadan Presence [74]. There is another foundational theme in Ibn Arabī's prophetology that stems from the first, and which Jīlī feels is particularly important: the stringently universal nature of the Prophet's soteriological role, which assures the entire human race – at least at the very end – of divine pardon. [75].

On the second point, regarding the initiatory domain, Jīlī's work further develops and expands on Ibn Arabī's. For Ibn Arabī, the idea of living life in imitation of the Prophet's actions is certainly foundational, but to a certain extent this goes without saying. What I mean by this is that, in the sense that it forms the bedrock for all his initiatory teaching, it pervades the entire corpus of his work. In this regard it is remarkable that chapter 560 of the *Futūhāt* – the chapter that brings the vast mystical summa to a close – is comprised especially of a long series of precepts drawn from the Sunna: a way for Ibn Arabī to tell his reader that all the knowledge and all the sciences addressed in the thousands of preceding pages can be discovered in, and extracted from, the strictest conformity to the Muhammadan model that constitutes their living source.

In fact, *ittibāʿ al-nabī* is not only the Shaykh al-Akbar's *sine qua non* condition for engagement in the search for God, it is also, and above all, the sole route of access to the highest degree of sanctity:

> When God allows Himself to be seen in the mirror of your
> heart, your mirror is only reflecting Him to the extent of its

capacity, and depending on its make up; [...] so persevere in faith and observance of the Prophetic model [*ittibā*] and *place the Prophet before you*, like a mirror [...], for the manifestation of God in the Prophet's mirror is the most perfect, the most exact, and the most beautiful. When you perceive Him in the Prophet's mirror, you are perceiving a perfection that you are unable to perceive if contemplating Him in your own mirror [...] Do not thus seek to contemplate God anywhere other than in the mirror of the Prophet, upon him be Grace and Peace. Beware of contemplating Him in your own mirror, or of contemplating the Prophet and what might be seen in his mirror via your own mirror [...] Persist in imitating him and in following him, and do not step into any place where you do not see the footprints of the Prophet. Place your foot in the place that was his if you wish to be among those who reach the highest of degrees and sublime contemplation [...] [76]

In the long *Futūhāt* chapter on "The Abode of Love" Ibn Arabī meditates on "divine words" (that is, on a *hadīth qudsī*) that he is particularly fond of. The hadith in question says "[...] and when I love him, I am the ear by which he hears, the sight by which he sees, the hand with which he grasps" [77]. This is why he is so adamant that it is solely *by means of*, and in, *ittibāʿ al-nabī* that the spiritual seeker can reach the station where God is his hearing, his sight, and so forth [78].

Jīlī's teaching on the matter is different, in the sense of its being, in contrast to Ibn Arabī, collected together and concentrated into a few works. Therein resides one of the key differences between Ibn Arabī's prophetocentric teachings and the prophetocentrism we see in Jīlī's works. The theme of the Prophet's preeminence, seen through its many aspects, runs throughout Ibn Arabi's work from beginning to end. But despite his devoting passages here and there to doctrinal ideas, none of his writings deals exclusively with this question. For Jīlī, it is not a question only of one recurrent theme among others, but rather of the central motif that brings order to the entirety of his work (which is, moreover, of much more modest proportions than Ibn Arabī's). In addition, Jīlī devoted several of his works, and not the least important of them, to meditations on the theme of the supreme perfection of the Prophet. Such was the case not only for the *Kamālāt*, but also, we should remember, for the best known of his works, the *Insān kāmil*,

"The Perfect Man," always meaning for him, as he tells us [79], the Prophet himself. And last, but not least, was the *Nāmūs*, Jīlī's magnum opus, in my opinion, which unfortunately is only very partially extant. Two of the seven treatises known still to exist are especially worthy of interest for our topic here. The first of these is *Nasīm al-sahar*, about which I will make a few short comments; the other is the *Qāb qawsayn*, which will be analyzed in greater length because of its importance as a leading account regarding the issue of devotion to the prophet.

"AND YOU WILL BE REUNITED WITH THE COMPANIONS" [80]

Nasīm al-sahar is one short chapter (the *Nāmūs*'s twelfth) with twelve sections, each of which refers back either to a specific event in the life of the Prophet (his retreat on Mount Hira, his watching over flocks of sheep, his trip to Syria) or to one of the main character traits of his personality (his love of women, perfume, prayer, and so forth). The chapter is in no way anything like a short "Life of the Prophet" (*sīra nabawiyya*), in the way that term might normally be understood. What Jīlī is engaging in here is a hermeneutics of the Prophet's biography, in an attempt to tease out its major spiritual meanings and thus encourage wayfarers to follow in the footprints of the Chosen One – that is, to model their behavior on the speech and behavior of the Prophet in regard to spiritual states.

The concept of *ittibāʿ al-nabī* is also central to the *Qāb qawsayn*, but seen this time from the perspective of a quite specific cultural practice, that of "attachment to the Prophet"; it moreover fits into a broad doctrinal expose where it appears as the final stage. Relative to Jīlī's other known works, the *Qāb qawsayn* is specific in the way it offers a complete and ordered summary of his teachings regarding the Prophet. All themes having anything to do with Muhammad get addressed: his primogeniture, his driving role in the cosmological process, his ontological status as *nuskhat al-haqq* ("image of God"), his universal role as spiritual teacher, his role as spiritual guide in the process of initiation, and so forth. In this regard, the *Qāb qawsayn* corresponds perfectly to what Jīlī was foreseeing when he began composing the *Nāmūs*, which he hoped would be "An eternal summa of knowledge regarding the eminence of the Prophet" [81].

The treatise is based on seven chapters, with Jīlī making it clear that the number was not chosen at random [82]. The reader might be expected to see it in connection with Jīlī's vision in Zabīd, where in 796 the Prophet appeared dressed in the seven divine entitative attributes. He also tells us that the work's title was inspired by God [83]. Let us remember that the expression *qāb qawsayn*, "at a distance of two bows," has its origin in the Qur'an, in Sura 53, the first eighteen verses of which are allusive references to the Prophet's "ascension" (*miʿrāj*) toward God, where he was ultimately led into His presence "at a distance of two bows, or closer" (*qāb qawsayn aw adnā*, 53:9). This scene from the Qur'an happened to play a role in a whole mystical hermeneutics that Ismāʿīl Haqqī (d. 1137/1725) would echo in the beautiful pages of his commentary on the Qur'an [84].

But in no way was it Jīlī's intention to do an exegesis of the verse in question here, even if, as will be seen, the meanings he offers for the expression *qāb qawsayn* – which he does not reveal until the end of the work – coincide to a certain degree with the interpretation that Muslim mystics offer for this important episode in the Prophet's spiritual journey. The goal he set for himself was of quite a different nature: to lift the veil off the secrets and the mysteries of the dazzling figure that the Prophet was, so that those questing after God might be encouraged to seek Him nowhere other than in the one who is His resplendent manifestation. He asserts that:

> There is no access to supreme felicity but through his intervention, [...] What is thus required is your attachment to his sublime presence and your locking onto the "Solid Bond" [85] – by virtue of his unsurpassable dignity, all the while never ceasing to hold in mind the perfect form that embraces all realities and forms of existence, to the point where the secrets spill the beverage of his love out over your spirit and your spirit over your heart and your heart over your soul and your soul over your body: a subtle beverage which revivifies both spirit and body, annihilating the contours of your individuality *to the point where you leave, and where he, upon him be Grace and Peace, is in you in lieu of yourself* [*fatadhhabūn wa yakūnu fīkum ʿiwādan minkum ʿankum*] [86].

There is another noteworthy passage in the introduction, the one constituting the first lines of the *khutba*, the "doxology" properly speaking, where from the outset Jīlī asserts that the Prophet is the place of epiphany for the divine essence – while the saints and the other prophets are the receptacles for divine attributes. This is a recurring theme in Jīlī's prophetology, appearing time after time, especially in two of the doxologies that lead into each of the sections of the *Nasīm* [87], and in the first chapter of the *Kamālāt* [88], as well as in a poem in *al-Kahf wa l-raqīm*, where Jīlī proclaims: "Messenger of God, o receptacle of Deity, you whose essence is pure essence! [*yā majlā l-ulūha wa yā man dhātuhu al-dhātu al-nazīha*]" [89].

The first five chapters of *Qāb qawsayn* pick up the essential themes of Ibn Arabī's Muhammadology, though in a style more fitting for Jīlī – more discursive, both lyrical and attention grabbing. The first chapter thus echoes the *'Anqā* pages where Ibn Arabī, meditating on the famous hadith "I was a hidden treasure and I loved to be known..." [90], depicts the divine drama that engendered Creation [91]: in reply to the urgent calls of the Divine Names pleading to be able to manifest themselves, God created the "Muhammadan Reality," the "image of God" (*nuskhat al-haqq*), and – Jīlī once again tells us – the epiphany of His essence.

The second chapter quickly touches on the idea of the Prophet's primogeniture ("the first thing God created..."), and that of his spiritual supremacy, before describing the long cosmological process for which the "Muhammadan Reality" is both the point of departure and what sets the universe into motion: a theme to which both the *Marātib al-wujūd*, and the forty-second chapter of *al-Insān al-kāmil* are entirely devoted.

Chapter three, which addresses the Prophet's perfection – both formal (*sūratan*) and subtle (*ma'nan*) – returns to, and summarizes, chapter three of the *Kamālāt*. In it, Jīlī thus reiterates his theory that the Prophet takes on all the Divine Names, with no exception, and then, in a second section, cites extensively a long hadith that gives a detailed description of the Prophet's physical appearance, all for the purpose, he finally tells us,

> of allowing you to imagine this noble constitution and to look upon it at each moment until it becomes present for you. In so doing, you will reach the rank of those who contemplate it, you will obtain supreme felicity, and you will *again find yourself among the Companions*, may God be satisfied with them all. And if you are not able to do this permanently, you should at least make that noble form present in all its perfection when you recite the *tasliya* [92].

The question of the Prophet's spiritual supremacy lies at the center of chapter four. This is Jīlī's opportunity, one more time, to assert that, by virtue of his ontological preeminence, the Prophet (and he alone) possesses the ability to "manifest God fully" (*qābiliyya kulliyya*), while all other creatures have a necessarily partial (*juz'iyya*) capacity for epiphany. The issue regarding the relationship between what belongs to the domain of "prophecy" (*nubuwwa*) and what to "sainthood" (*walāya*) is also addressed, from a perspective typical of the Shaykh al-Akbar.

In a fifth chapter, Jīlī offers a long meditation on the *hadīth qudsī* mentioned earlier, "I was a hidden treasure and I loved to be known..." He interprets the hadith in the way that Ibn Arabī had done in his *Kitāb al-hujub*, positing that Creation was initially an act of love [93], the object of this love being the Prophet, or more precisely, the object of this love being the "Muhammadan Reality" that is thus the "first cause" (*asl*) through which the universe came into being and the final cause for its existentiation. This is specifically explained by the famous tradition "Were it not for you, I would not have created the universe"; the hadith's authenticity has been seriously questioned, although Jīlī relies on its support. What then follows is a long passage that looks like an abbreviated version of chapter 178 of the *Futūhāt*, on "the abode of love," where Ibn Arabī enumerates the many degrees of love.

With chapters six and seven we reach the part of *Qāb qawsayn* that is by far the most remarkable, and the most meaningful; when we realize this, it becomes easier to understand why Muhammad al-Sammān might have given in to the temptation to plagiarize it. In contrast to several doctrinal statements in his earlier chapters, Jīlī is here developing trains of thought never found in Ibn Arabī nor, to my knowledge, in any earlier writer. The underlying concept for this section – that of "attachment" (*ta'alluq*) to the Prophet – is of course not new; as we have seen, it was explained, albeit briefly, in the writings of Ahmad al-Wāsitī, who died a century before Jīlī did.

After an early reminder of the spiritual seeker's need to strive to gather divine grace through the intervention of the Muhammadan receptacle, Jīlī proceeds more deeply to describe the two modalities of this attachment to the Prophet: formal (*sūrī*) attachment and subtle (*ma'nawī*) attachment. The former rests on two principles. First, it requires strict observance of precepts in both the Qur'an and the Sunna, while also conforming to the prescriptions of one of the four Sunni schools of jurisprudence. Secondly, it implies "following the Prophet and loving him strongly" (*an tattabi'ahu bi shiddat al-mahabba*), about which Jīlī tells of his personal experience:

> By God, what my love for him makes me feel in my heart, in my spirit, in my body, in every hair and in my skin is analogous to what I experience in my being at my very first contact with water when, in great thirst, I take it in on a day of intense heat. [...] I, who darken these pages, God's poor servant 'Abd al-Karīm b. Ibrāhīm b. 'Abd al-Karīm b. Khalīfa b. Ahmad b. Mahmūd al-Kaylānī [94] al-Baghdādī al-Rabīʿī al-Sūfī, take God as my witness – as well as His angels, His prophets and His messengers and all His creatures – that I love Muhammad, the Messenger of God, that I prefer him to my own soul, to my spirit, to my possessions and my child. The love that I feel toward him makes me feel in my heart, in my body, in my every hair and in my skin a flowing and a current so tangible that no one who has felt it could deny [95].

As with formal attachment, there are also two kinds of subtle attachment. The first consists in bringing to mind the bodily appearance of the Prophet according to the well-defined modalities outlined by Jīlī in a passage that probably was the treatise's culmination:

> His apparent form should be permanently held in mind as it was previously described, while observing the proper rules and showing veneration, reverence, and a respectful fear. And if you are incapable of creating a mental image of his form as thus described, but have seen it in your sleep, then imagine it in the form you saw in your sleep. And if you have never seen it in your sleep and find yourself incapable of seeing it as previously described, mention it, and recite the *tasliya*, and behave as if you were in his presence when he was alive, with reverence, veneration, and respectful fear, for he sees you and he hears you each time you mention him [...] And if you cannot remain thusly in his presence but you have had occasion to visit his noble tomb, to see the *rawda* and the cupola, then mentally call upon the image of his tomb, and each time you mention him and you recite prayer upon him, do it as if you were standing before his tomb with veneration and respect, until such point that you perceive his spiritual presence [*rūhāniyyatahu*]. And if you have not visit-

ed his tomb and have not seen the *rawda*, recite the prayer upon him unceasingly while imagining that he hears you, with respect and concentration so that your prayer might reach him...[96]

At this point we should turn our attention back to a text mentioned earlier: the famous passage where Sanūsī describes the essential practice that the "Muhammadan Way" is based on. Some have considered the work to be foundational, in the sense that it was introducing a previously unknown practice that opened a new current in *tasawwuf*: prophetocentrism.

The second form of subtle attachment is not unlike apprehension of the Prophet's essential reality (*haqīqatuhu*). As Jīlī remarks, this assumes that one knows he is the "isthmus" (*barzakh*) between the eternal and the contingent, referring – he specifies – to the Qur'anic expression *qāb qawsayn aw adnā* [97]. Like several others before him (most notably Ibn Arabī), Jīlī is referring here to the symbolism of the circle split in half by a median, where each half-circle becomes an arc. The upper half-circle is Eternal Being, *haqq*; the lower half-circle is *khalq*, contingent beings; the median – which simultaneously separates and conjoins them, thus sharing the nature of each – is the "Muhammadan Reality" [98].

In chapter 427 of the *Futūhāt* [99], dealing with the interpretation of this verse from Sura 53, Ibn Arabī also uses the image of a circle to illustrate the exceptional spiritual status of the Prophet, though he does so from a perspective different from what Jīlī had in mind. Here, the median drawing a distinction between *haqq* and the *khalq* (the "Real" and the "creatural") is nothing other than the creature's "I." This "I" – in that it posits the autonomous existence of an individual – is illusory, since only God has being. It is consequently only at the price of a *mors mystica* – in Meister Eckhart's sense of the term, constituting the highest degree of full and complete annihilation of the ego – that theosis takes place. It is at this point that the illusory line of demarcation that, like a mirage, was reflecting two arcs and consequently reflecting a duality, disappears; all that remains is the single circle of the One, with no second [100]. "The [true] believer is he who has sold his soul (*man bā'a nafsahu*)," Ibn Arabī abruptly declares in a passage in the *Futūhāt*; "from that point on, all that remains in him is someone (*man*) who can demand [whatever]" [101]. And it is precisely to this spiritual station – that of the highest and most perfect proximity that could possibly exist – that, according to Ibn Arabī, the expression *aw adnā* is referring in the Sura 53 passage regarding the Prophet's spiritual ascension.

In the seventh and last chapter, Jīlī mentions the fruits and spiritual benefits that accrue from the practice of *ta'alluq*. He cites a number of hadiths relating to the virtues of *tasliya*, and then envisions one somewhat peculiar case:

> One of the Prophet's claims to primacy is that when a saint sees him, during a theophany, clothed in one of the robes of perfection, the Prophet offers it to him, and thereafter it belongs to him. If the saint in question is sufficiently strong, he can don the robe immediately; if not, it is placed in reserve with God until he is strong enough to wear it, in this world or in the other. He who gets this robe and wears it, in this world or in the other, is getting it directly from the Prophet, and this is the height of moral character [*futuwwa*]. Whoever then has a vision of the saint clothed in the robe is, in turn, offered the robe by the saint, on behalf of the Prophet. As a replacement, the saint receives another robe, more perfect than the first. And if a third person subsequently has a vision of the second beneficiary, the same event will again occur, and so on indefinitely [102].

An examination of the *Qāb qawsayn* makes clear that the prophetocentrism characterizing doctrinal and initiatory teachings of Sufi masters in the 18th and 19th centuries is in no way a novel phenomenon that arose out of who knows where. Not that we therefore need to see Jīlī as the founding father of the Muhammadan Way. Doing so would mean forgetting that, in every era since the earliest days of Islam, the quest for God is mixed in with *ittibā' al-nabī* in the strict sense of the term, and that it implies following, step by step and patiently, the itinerary trodden by God's Chosen One, for the truth is that his path is, to use Hīrī's expression, "the ideal path." In my opinion, there is no doubt that the practice of *ta'alluq*, even if we do not see specific wording in texts until the 13th century, was in common use among those who, in one era or another, aspired to be Companions of the Prophet.

The fact remains that Jīlī's work marks an important point in the development of devotion to the Prophet as a doctrinal theme, a theme that has continued to spread with the passing of centuries. Of all his writings, the *Qāb qawsayn* is remarkable, distilling into a few pages both the *doctrinal motifs* that underpin and lay foundations for this prophetocentric concept of sanctity, and *ritual practices*. The practices are quite simple, yet they allow the practitioner access to *suhba*, meaning that he is able to benefit both effectively and immediately from the "company" of the Teacher par excellence: from him who was, is, and forever remains "the Perfect Man."

Notes:
[1] Qur'an 53:9.
[2] IBN AL-AHDAL, 1964, p. 214.
[3] SHARJĪ, 1321 A.H., note regarding Ibn al-Raddād, p. 30, and regarding Jabartī, pp. 37-40; cf. also the note on p. 170, regarding Jabartī's disciple Muhammad al-Ashkal, who composed a large volume on his teacher's *karamāt* (ASHKAL, 2008) that at several points referred to Jīlī's oral testimony, which he thus knew.
[4] Cf. ATLAGH, 2000, pp. 17-18.
[5] This poem appears after the colophon for a manuscript of the *Ghunyat arbāb al-samā*, ms., folio 296; cf. ATLAGH, 2000, pp. 17-18.
[6] Cf. ATLAGH, 2000, pp. 18-21.
[7] JĪLĪ, 1970, 2nd part, p. 53.
[8] ID., 1985, p. 28.
[9] ID., 1970, 1st part, p. 97.
[10] *Ibid.*, 2nd part, p. 97.
[11] Qur'an 64:8. Jīlī, 2004, p. 125; R. Atlagh prepared a critical edition of the *Kamālāt*. I was able to consult it, though it was not published.
[12] ATLAGH, 2000, p. 20.
[13] JĪLĪ, 2004, p. 14.
[14] ATLAGH, 2000, p. 20.
[15] JĪLĪ, 2004, p. 170.
[16] ATLAGH, 2000, p. 104.
[17] KNYSH, 1997, pp. 241-246; SHARJĪ, 1321 A.H., pp. 37-40.
[18] YAHIA, 1964, II, p. 541; IBN ARABĪ, n.d., p. 135; ID., 2006, p. 20 (chain F), 25.
[19] ZABĪDĪ, ms. (b), folio 16.
[20] IBN HAJAR AL-'ASQALĀNĪ, 1968-1972, II, p. 272.
[21] JĪLĪ, 2005 (b), p. 38.
[22] KHAZRAJĪ, 1983, II, p. 248.
[23] On relations between Rasūlid rulers and Sufis, cf. KNYSH, 1997, ch. IX.
[24] *EI2*, "Rasūlids."
[25] KNYSH, 1997, p. 242.
[26] This sovereign abdicated the toward the end of his life, passing power to his son. According to KHAZRAJĪ, 1983, I, pp. 232-233, he was well versed in both hadith and *tafsīr*.
[27] According to AL-QĀRĪ AL-BAGHDĀDĪ, 1959, p. 64, al-Nāsir possessed a great number of Ibn Arabī's works.
[28] KHAZRAJĪ, 1983, II, p. 197.

[29] *EI2*, "Fīrūzābādī."

[30] The wording of the fatwa was reproduced in AL-QĀRĪ AL-BAGHDĀDĪ, 1959, pp. 64-72.

[31] KNYSH, 1997, pp. 246-261.

[32] ATLAGH, 2000, p. 22.

[33] Of the seven treatises extant, three have been printed in their entirety: the *Qāb qawsayn*, redone in NABHĀNĪ, 1998, IV, pp. 261-264, and in BURHĀNĪ (d. 1983), n.p., n.d., pp. 44-67 (notes refer to this edition); the *Nasīm al-sahar*, published in Cairo, n.d., and later in a collection (JĪLĪ, 2005 [a], pp. 65-106) which included a number of other treatises, including the *Marātib al-wujūd* (ID., 2005 [b], pp. 36-62), and also reproduced in NABHĀNĪ, 1998, IV, pp. 290-310; and finally the *Lawāmiʿ al-barq*, 2010. The *Kitāb sirr al-nūr al-munkamin* was only partially reproduced in NABHĀNĪ, 1998, IV, p. 284-290.

[34] ATLAGH, 2000, pp. 59-60.

[35] Published in French under the title *De l'homme universel* (JĪLĪ, 1975).

[36] Jīlī's criticism of Ibn Arabī can be seen in chapters 17, 18, and 19.

[37] CHODKIEWICZ, 2002.

[38] *Ibid.*, note 41. Jīlī's case is similar to that of Sitt ʿAjam, who followed Ibn Arabī's orders to write a commentary on his *Mashāhid*, and yet took the liberty of criticizing it condescendingly (SITT, 2004, pp. 16, 222, 250, 362).

[39] IBN ARABĪ, 1911, II, pp. 24, 324.

[40] *Ibid.*, III, p. 251.

[41] JĪLĪ, 1985, p. 28 says 799, but the Berlin manuscript (we 1631, folio 222a) says 796; the latter is corroborated by an indication in ID., 1970, 2nd part, p. 74.

[42] Let us remember that this verse is traditionally interpreted as referring to the seven verses of the *Fātiha* (TABARĪ, n.d., VII, 14th part, pp. 36-42).

[43] Qurʾan 68:4.

[44] JĪLĪ, 1992, p. 174, points out that the *haqīqa muhammadiyya* was created ʿalā l-nuskhat al-ilāhiyya.

[45] We find an analogous interpretation in Ruzbehān Baqlī, though Baqlī's is in regard to verse 68:4 ("In truth, you are of a sublime nature"), to which he connects Aʾisha's famous hadith that we saw in a previous chapter: "His nature was the Qurʾan" (BALLANFAT, 2002, p. 213, note 44).

[46] This concerns the *Nafāʾis al-ʿirfān*, published in IBN ARABĪ, 1967, p. 21 (cf. YA-HIA, 1964, II, "Répertoire général des oeuvres d'Ibn Arabî," 519; McGREGOR, 2007). Several of M. Wafāʾs treatises have been attributed to Ibn Arabī because he depended so much on him (cf. for example, ""Répertoire général des oeuvres d'Ibn Arabî," 148, 417, 663, 803, 815). We might also note that the thousand-verse *Tāʾiyya* attributed to Ibn Arabī under two titles, *ibid.*, 211 and 566, was actually by Wafā. On Wafā and his son ʿAlī (d. 807/1404) – a contemporary of Jīlī and who thus could have met him during his stay in Cairo – cf. the excellent monograph by McGREGOR, 2004. The Wafās' attitude – both father and son heavily borrowed from Ibn Arabī's terminology and teachings without ever crediting him – was not dissimilar to that of Ibn Sabʿin (CHOD-KIEWICZ, 2002, note 40).

[47] IBN ARABĪ, 1954, p. 38.

[48] Muhammad Demirdāsh (ob. 929/1523) devoted a treatise to commentary on verse 15:87 in which he proposed an exegesis that very closely mirrors Jīlī's (CHODKIEWICZ, 2004, pp. 22-25 and note 36).

[49] For example, we see a similar allusion to *mithl* in IBN ARABĪ, 1988, p. 52.

[50] The absence of repercussions and, consequently, of persecutions, can be explained by the fact that – other than the *Insān kāmil* – Jīlī's works lay in the shadows for a long time, having been distributed to a relatively limited number of individuals. It is however notable that the publication of BURHĀNĪ (d. 1983), n.d., a publication that included Jīlī's *Qāb qawsayn*, did give rise to lively debate, and its author was accused of deifying the Prophet (HOFFMAN, 1995, ch. 10).

[51] JĪLĪ, 2004, p. 11.

[52] *Ibid.*, p. 104. The more reliable text established by Atlagh (p. 62) says: *famaʿrifatuhu li Llāh ʿayn maʿrifati Llāh linafsihi.*

[53] *Ibid.*, p. 135.

[54] *Ibid.*, p. 126.

[55] *Ibid.*, p. 125. In citing this Qurʾanic verse, Jīlī has it introduced not by the sacred phrase "God, may He be exalted, said...," but rather by "he [the Prophet], upon him be Grace and Peace, said..." Was this really a "slip"? It certainly was not, in the sense that this passage immediately precedes the one where he affirms that "the Qurʾan is the word of the Prophet."

[56] CHODKIEWICZ, 1994 (a), pp. 24-25; GRIL, 2005, p. 139.

[57] Qurʾan 34:28.

[58] Cf. above, ch. 2, pp. 40ff.

[59] For "*law lāka,*" cf. JĪLĪ, 2004, p. 20, BURHĀNĪ, n.d., n.p., p. 59. Regarding the hadith "The first thing God created was," Jīlī mentions all the existing versions in no apparent order: *al-qalam, al-ʿaql, nūr nabiyyika, nūrī, rūh nabiyyika, rūhī.* Cf. JĪLĪ, 1992, p. 67 (*rūh nabiyyika, qalam, ʿaql*); ID., 1985, pp. 6, 27 (*rūh nabiyyika*); ID., ms. (a) reproduced by BURHĀNĪ, n.d. n.p., p. 48 (*rūh, qalam, ʿaql*); JĪLĪ, 2005 (b), p. 47 (*nūr nabiyyika*); ID., ms. (b) folio 42a (*nūrī, rūhī, rūh nabiyyika*). Emir ʿAbd al-Qādir did likewise (ʿABD AL-QĀDIR AL-JAZĀ'IRĪ, 1966, especially I, pp. 181, 182, 183, 185, II, pp. 631, 645).

[60] GRIL, 2005.

[61] ʿAJLŪNĪ, 1351 A.H., num. 619. Emir ʿAbd al-Qādir cited this version (ʿABD AL-QĀDIR AL-JAZĀ'IRĪ, 1966, I, p. 186).

[62] JĪLĪ, 2004, p. 19; ID., 1985, p. 29; ID., n.d. n.p., p. 48; ID., 2005 (a), p. 88.

[63] ID., 1985, p. 15.

[64] Emir ʿAbd al-Qādir mentions this tradition (ʿABD AL-QĀDIR AL-JAZĀ'IRĪ, 1966, I, p. 445).

[65] This idea was also addressed in IBN ARABĪ, 1911, IV, p. 161; ID., 1954, pp. 50-51, although without mentioning this hadith.

[66] JĪLĪ, 2004, p. 125.

[67] This term denotes the space in the mosque in Medina between the Prophet's tomb and the minbar (the pulpit). A *rawda* is, according to a hadith, "a garden among the gardens of Paradise," but it will only appear thus to the *ʿārif bi-Llāh.*

[68] Qurʾan 53:7.

[69] Qur'an 112:1.
[70] JĪLĪ, 2004, p. 14.
[71] *Ibid.*
[72] Qur'an 68:4.
[73] JĪLĪ, 2004, p. 125.
[74] On these two points, cf. CHODKIEWICZ, 1986, ch. 4 and 5.
[75] See above, ch. 4, pp. 67ff.
[76] IBN ARABĪ, 1911, III, pp. 251-252. This passage is largely reproduced in a small work falsely attributed to Ibn Arabī, titled *al-Tanbīhāt 'alā 'uluw l-haqīqa al-muhammadiyya*, Cairo, 1987, pp. 33-34, a treatise also reproduced in NABHĀNĪ, 1998, IV, pp. 311-320 (italics mine).
[77] On this famous hadith, cf. CHODKIEWICZ, 1982, pp. 202-203, note 84.
[78] IBN ARABĪ, 1911, II, p. 341.
[79] JĪLĪ, 1970, 2nd part, p. 72; ID., ms. (c), folio 181a.
[80] ID., n.d.n.p., p. 55.
[81] The complete title of the *Nāmūs* is *al-Nāmūs al-a'zam wa l-qāmūs al-aqdam fī ma'rifati qadri al-nabī.*
[82] ID., n.d.n.p., p. 46.
[83] *Ibid.*, p. 47.
[84] HAQQĪ, n.d., IX, pp. 208-232.
[85] Qur'an 2:256, 31:22.
[86] JĪLĪ, n.d.n.p., p. 46 (italics mine).
[87] ID., 2005 (a), pp. 65, 86.
[88] ID., 2004, p. 19.
[89] ID., 1985, p. 28.
[90] This *hadith qudsī* appears to have been put into circulation somewhat late (cf. H. Landolt's detailed note in ISFARĀYINĪ, 1986, p. 202, note 60). According to Isfarāyinī, God's words were addressed to David (*ibid.*, p. 156). IBN ARABĪ, 1991, indicates that it appeared in one of the revealed books, without offering further details, although in his 1911 publication, II, p. 399, he claims that he learned via a revelation that the hadith was authentic. Cf. also 'AJLŪNĪ, 1351 A.H., num. 2016.
[91] IBN ARABĪ, 1954, pp. 32-40.
[92] JĪLĪ, n.d.n.p., p. 55 (italics mine).
[93] IBN ARABĪ, 1991, p. 39. Cf. also ADDAS, 2002, p. 132.
[94] According to the vocalization offered in JĪLĪ, m.s. (a), folio 35.
[95] *Ibid.*, n.d.n.p., p. 63.
[96] *Ibid.*, p. 64.
[97] Qur'an 53:9.
[98] JĪLĪ, n.d.n.p., p. 65.
[99] IBN ARABĪ, 1911, IV, pp. 39-40.
[100] This is also the interpretation according to HAQQĪ, n.d., IX, p. 219.
[101] IBN ARABĪ, 1911, III, p. 471.
[102] JĪLĪ, n.d.n.p., p. 67.

Chapter Eight

The House of the Prophet

"THE PEOPLE OF MY HOUSE ARE A SAFEGUARD FOR MY COMMUNITY" [1]

Ahlu baytī amān li ummatī, "The people of My House are a safe-guard for My Community." Though not appearing in any of the canonical collections [2], this statement attributed to the Prophet is one of the countless traditions [3] that lie at the base of Muslim believers' veneration of the *ahl al-bayt* [4], the "family of the Prophet" in the broad sense of the term; in this sense, the term includes the *shurafā*, the Prophet's descendants through his daughter Fātima. The words *ahl al-bayt* actually appear twice in the Qur'an [5], once concerning the family around the Prophet (verse 33 of Sura *al-Ahzāb*), saying: "God wants only to separate you from uncleanliness, o People of the House, and to purify you fully."

It goes without saying that exactly who these *ahl al-bayt* were has been the subject of unending debate. Among Sunni commentators alone, I might note that for some – most notably, the illustrious Tabarī – *ahl al-bayt* in this verse should be understood to include, in addition to the Prophet himself, his daughter Fātima, his cousin and son-in-law 'Alī, and his two grandsons Hasan and Hussayn [6]; in other words, those who also tend to be understood as the *ahl al-kisā*, "the People of the Cloak," in reference to the "event of Mubahala," alluded to in verse 61 of the third Sura [7].

Other commentators, one of whom is Ibn Kathīr (d. 774/1373), are nevertheless of the opinion that the "context" (*siyāq al-kalām*) surrounding this verse would require that the Prophet's wives also be included, since it is they who are directly addressed in the preceding verses and in the verse that follows [8].

This latter interpretation is also held by Hakīm Tirmidhī, the author of the *Khatm al-awliyā* ("Seal of the Saints"), mentioned in the previous chapter [9]. An ardent defender of Sunni Islam, Tirmidhī never missed a chance to vent his deep disagreement with Shi'ite beliefs regarding the power of the caliph, although this did not keep him (as was also the case for a number of *tasawwuf* masters, and particularly Ibn Arabī) from praising 'Alī's spiritual excellence.

Tirmidhī thus devoted an entire chapter in his *Nawādir al-usūl*, a collection of prophetic traditions, to discussing the idea of *ahl al-bayt*, with the point of departure for his thoughts being precisely the hadith *Ahlu baytī amān li ummatī* [10]. The entire scope of the hadith – we might even call it a prediction – actually rests on the way one interprets the expression *ahlu baytī*, the "People of my House." And Tirmidhī cannot be more categorical on this point: *ahlu baytī* does denote the Prophet's lineage, but it also includes the line of saints who have reached the highest degree of spiritual realization, *whether or not they they are blood relatives descending from the Messenger.* It is these "men of God" in the strongest sense of that term that he singles out as the "True Ones" (*siddiqūn*), or as the "Pillars" (*awtād*). It is they who are the guardians of the *umma*, the "Community of the Prophet." It is, moreover, thanks to them that humanity is able to survive [11].

We see easily why the theory Tirmidhī is espousing here – which runs counter to the common opinion that *ahlu baytī* refers to the Prophet's family in the strictest sense of the term – has given rise to serious disagreement, including among his admirers. This was most notably the case for Nabhānī, who, the day after *Nawādir al-usūl* was published [12], was taken aside by a Meccan *sharīf* wanting him to reject Tirmidhī's statements about the matter, and to do so in writing [13]. Nabhānī initially dithered; he had never written before, and did not feel worthy of the mission. Even more so, this presented a serious dilemma: yes, Tirmidhī was wrong about this specific point, and there was no doubt in his mind about this; but Nabhānī was equally convinced that Tirmidhī was a saint, and one of the greatest. This was at least the opinion of a teacher for whom Nabhānī had the utmost reverence, a teacher he did not hesitate to refer to as the *shaykh al-akbar*, "the greatest of teachers," Ibn Arabī. After considerable reflection, Nabhānī finally did consent to the "request" with the first of a long series of works, many of which were devoted to the figure of Prophet and the veneration that is his due. He did so by refuting Tirmidhī's interpretation, albeit, he stressed, without showing any lack of respect.

What Nabhānī was not aware of – at least, perhaps, he pretended not to be aware of it [14] – was that Ibn Arabī was broadly in

agreement with Tirmidhī's point of view about what *ahl al-bayt* referred to, as he actually was with a number of his other views. One
difference, however, was that Ibn Arabī's concept of the "Muhammadan family" contained doctrinal nuances not present in either
Tirmidhī's *Nawādir* or his *Khatm al-awliyā'*, both of which address
the issue [15].

One lexical issue should be resolved before going more deeply into this subject. We know that, in his hermeneutics, Ibn Arabī
placed extreme importance on the examination of religious vocabulary, both in the Qur'an and in hadith [16]. In this present
case, he emphasizes the difference between the words *ahl* and *āl*;
the two are more or less synonyms in current usage. I might point
out that the word *āl* is the one used in the *tasliya*, the "prayer on
the Prophet" – at least in its earliest form – where it is generally
understood as meaning "family," just as is the case for *ahl*. This
is, however, not correct in Ibn Arabī's opinion, as he says: "Do
not get the idea that the term *āl Muhammad* is referring to the
"People of his House"; this is not the way the Arabs use it" [17].
He also says "In the Arabic language, the saying *āl al-rajul* denotes
an individual's family and others close to him." As evidence, the
Futūhāt's author relies on the Qur'anic use of the word, and specifically on verse 46 of the fourth Sura: "Send *those close to the
Pharaoh* (*āl fir'awn*) into the worst of punishments." Evidently, *āl*
is not referring to the Pharaoh's relatives strictly speaking here,
but rather to the close advisors who supported the way he used
his power and were thereby complicit in its misuse. In the same
way, he says in regard to the prophets, the word *āl* should be understood as referring to those who were the closest to them in
faith, meaning the "pious-gnostic-believers" (*al-sālihūn al-'ārifūn
al-mu'minūn*) [18]. So, when the faithful believer calls for divine
grace when reciting the *tasliya*, it is being called to fall upon these
"men of God" and not just upon the Prophet's blood relatives.
The practice of *tasliya*, it should be remembered, was instituted
after the revelation of verse 56 in Sura *al-Ahzāb*: "God and His
angels bless the Prophet. O you who believe, invoke God's blessings upon the Prophet and call for Peace upon him." Asked by his
Companions about how they carry out this directive, the Prophet
replied: "Say: Lord, blessed be Muhammad and *those close* to Muhammad (*āl Muhammad*), as You blessed Abraham and *those close*
to Abraham (*āl Ibrāhīm*)" [19].

In so doing, Ibn Arabī tells us, the Prophet was expanding the Qur'anic prescription by requiring believers to ask that the divine graces granted to "those close to Abraham" be similarly granted to "those close" to the Prophet himself [20]. To a number of those close to Abraham God had granted *nubuwwa*, the status of prophet, a status that – since it includes such actions as instituting laws (*nubuwwat al-tashrī*) – was beyond reach ever since the Messenger's death; he was after all, to use the Qur'an's expression *khātam l-nabiyyīn* [21], the "Seal of the prophets." From this perspective, no one after him would be able to claim *nubuwwa*; such is the message of the well-known hadith stating that no prophet or any messenger would arise after Muhammad [22].

However, this brings up an essential issue in Ibn Arabī's hagiological doctrine: prophecy was not limited to the exercise of magistrature. It also implied the development of an eminent degree of spiritual perfection, and when looked at from this specific perspective, the concept of *nubuwwa* referred to a "spiritual station" (*maqām*), the highest of all – which Ibn Arabī sometimes called the "station of general prophecy" (in contrast to "lawgiving prophecy"), and sometimes the "station of proximity (*maqām al-qurba*) – and which *remains accessible to the most perfect of all the saints* [23]. Ibn Arabī's conclusion was that, in transmitting this specific wording for benediction to his Community, what the Prophet meant was that those among the '*ārifūn* who were "close to him" – the "gnostics" – might actually reach this supreme degree of sanctity, although they would not be able to exercise "lawgiving prophecy" (*nubuwwat al-tashrī*) [24].

The interpretation that Ibn Arabī offers for the expression *āl Muhammad* here differs considerably from what most of the ulama held, of course. As a matter of fact, this is not the only interpretation the Shaykh al-Akbar is known to have offered. Because Arabic is a polysemic language par excellence, and because Ibn Arabi's hermeneutics drew on everything semantics had to offer, another text from the *Futūhāt* envisioned a quite different, yet no less subtle, meaning.

Among the different entries for the word *āl* in the quite comprehensive encyclopedia of the Arabic language known as the *Lisān al-'arab* is that of *sarāb*, "mirage" [25]. This is the meaning that Ibn Arabī chose for the passage in question; it appears in the long section in chapter 73 where he offers a response to Tirmidhī's

"Questionnaire," which we discussed earlier [26]. In this case, it is in the one hundred fifty-first question: "What is the meaning of *āl Muhammad?*"

> *Āl* is what magnifies figures. In fact, *āl* is what we call the size of figures that appear in a mirage. *Āl Muhammad* are thus those who are magnified by Muhammad [*al-ʿuzamāʾ bi Muhammad*], and Muhammad, upon him be Grace and Peace, is like the mirage that makes whoever is seen in it appear to be immense. You therefore believe that it refers to Muhammad, with great stature, just as you believe that the mirage is water – and to the eye it actually appears to be water – but when you reach Muhammad, it is not him that you find, *it is God that you find in Muhammadan form, due to a Muhammadan vision* [27].

These few lines are dense from a doctrinal point of view, yet they express – albeit allusively – two key ideas in Ibn Arabī's initiatory teachings. The first of these is that each time we find ourselves in need of something, to whatever degree, this need – because it is an expression of our radical indigence, of our inability to be sufficient unto ourselves – reveals our need for "Him Who is sufficient unto Himself." It also serves as a call – though a silent one – addressed to the Eternal. And because theophanies necessarily take on the form of the receptacle in which they appear, when God answers this call it is invariably by revealing Himself in the form that is expected of Him. When he went off in search of fire, Moses found God in the form of the burning bush. In like manner, the man dying of thirst discovers Him where he hopes with all his heart and soul to find water [28]. Unquestionably then, he who goes off to follow in the Prophet's footsteps can be certain to find his Lord at his journey's conclusion. And in addition – and this is the second essential point of this passage – the seeker will have the most perfect knowledge of his Lord possible, for "the most perfect vision of God is that produced in the form of Muhammad by the Muhammadan form; I have never stopped encouraging people toward this, in my speaking and in this book" [29].

To the extent that the Prophet – or more precisely, the "Muhammadan Reality" that is his personification – is the perfect "image of God" (*nuskhat al-haqq*) and thus possesses all the divine attributes, "the knowledge that he has of God is the very knowledge that God has of Himself," to use Jīlī's words [30]. Consequently, it is by walking in the footsteps of the Prophet – that is, by adhering strictly to his "excellent model" (*uswa hasana*) that the pilgrim attains the highest knowledge of God.

Regardless of the meaning he ascribes to *āl* – "those close to," or "mirage" – Ibn Arabī clearly is not referring specifically to the Prophet's family, his blood relatives, when he says *āl Muhammad*.

What about the term *ahl al-bayt*? Ibn Arabī does offer an important hint to the answer in his *Jawāb mustaqīm* – where, as we saw earlier, he responds to Tirmidhī's "Questionnaire" point by point – and in chapter 73 of the *Futūhāt*, although here he is much more succinct. Thus, in answer to the question "What does his statement *Ahlu baytī amān li ummatī* [31] mean?", he merely answers by citing these words attributed to the Prophet: "Salmān is one of us, the "People of the House" (*Salmān minnā ahlu l-bayt*) [32].

The response is lapidary, to be sure, yet enlightening nevertheless. Salmān was an eminent Companion, but by no means a blood relative. He was, moreover, a foreigner, a "non-Arab" (*'ajamī*) [33]. It was thus Ibn Arabī's intention to point out that being related by blood is not, a priori, a *sine qua non* condition for claim to the privilege of membership in the Prophet's family. This then raises the question of what criteria, in his view, did define membership in the *ahl al-bayt*. Moreover, how did Ibn Arabī think the specific case of Salmān was relevant to this discussion?

The deliberately terse nature of the *Jawāb* aimed no doubt at nothing more than piquing its reader's curiosity, of encouraging the search for further information in the Shaykh al-Akbar's other works. Information relevant to this question is found in the *Futūhāt*'s twenty-ninth chapter, the title of which tells us that it deals with "The knowledge of Salmān's secret by virtue of which the Prophet attached him to the *ahl al-bayt* and that of the spiritual Poles to whom he was heir" [34]. In a very meaningful way, it was the theme of "pure servitude" (*'ubūdiyya mahda*) that Ibn Arabī was addressing primarily. When he uses the expression, it refers to the ultimate state of spiritual perfection, that of those saints who, following the example of the Prophet, freed themselves from any will of their own, from any creatures and any things, such that they fully realized the sentence from the *Futūhāt* that recapitulates the essentials of the Shaykh al-Akbar's teaching about this issue: "What God wants of you is for you to be with Him such as you were when you were not a thing" [35]. No more...no less. It goes without saying that only the most perfect of the saints (*awliyāʾ*) – those very saints who are admitted into the supreme "station of proximity" mentioned above – manage to reach this peak [36].

In any case, it is because the Prophet had fully and completely and in all respects realized this state of "perfect servitude" that, Ibn Arabi asserts, God reciprocated by granting both him and his family absolute "purification," as in the words of verse 33 in Sura *al-Ahzāb*, which we saw above: "God wants only to separate you from uncleanliness, o People of the House, and to purify you fully." It follows, as we are told by the *Futūhāt*'s author, that whoever is attached to the "People of the House" becomes thereby purified himself; otherwise, the Prophet's family would be stained by uncleanliness. Since the Prophet integrated Salmān into his family on purpose, Salmān necessarily enjoyed this prerogative granted to the *ahl al-bayt* [37]. Ibn Arabī nevertheless emphasizes – and this point is important because it shows that, on the issue of the *ahl al-bayt*'s innate preeminence, his point of view differs from that of Tirmidhī – that there is a difference between those who are purified by virtue of their attachment to the Prophet's family (Salmān's case is an example here, though not the only one, as we shall see) and the *ahl al-bayt* properly speaking, meaning those who are blood relatives of the Prophet. The latter, he maintains, "are the purified; what do I mean? They are the very essence of purity! (*Hum ʿayn al-tahāra*)" [38].

So be it. But just what, for Ibn Arabī, does the idea of *tathīr* ("purification") in Sura *al-Ahzāb* actually include? What, for him, are its consequences from a legal perspective? What attitude toward the *ahl al-bayt* does all this imply for the common believer? All these are issues that Ibn Arabī addresses, directly and in detail, in the text that follows; and given their close relevance to key themes of disagreement between Sunnis and Shiʿites, it is surprising that this chapter in the *Futūhāt* has not been more closely examined by those who would like to consider Ibn Arabī a "crypto-Shiʿite."

Whatever he might be, and more directly relevant to the first point, Ibn Arabī's position is unambiguous: *tathīr* is in this case a synonym for *ʿisma*, "impeccability" [39], a word pregnant with meaning for Sunni theologians but even more so for their Shiʿite brothers: it refers to the idea that prophets – and the Imams, from the Shiʿite perspective – are free from sin. In this sense, it is important to draw lines around what the concept actually includes for Ibn Arabī.

What is at first surprising is that, in the passages where he addresses the subject, the *Futūhāt*'s author is always referring to verse 2 of Sura *al-Fath* [40], a verse that seems paradoxically to invalidate teachings about impeccability, since it tells the Prophet that God has pardoned all his sins, both past and future: "*li yaghfira laka Llāh mā taqaddama min dhanbika wa mā ta'akhkhara.*" As we have seen, commentators usually skirt around the problem, arguing that the sins in question were "minor errors" (*saghā'ir*), committed inadvertently (*sahwan*) [41].

Ibn Arabī's hermeneutic procedure is quite different. As always, he first draws from the literal meaning, which reduces all the contradictions. What the verse states, he says, is that "divine pardon" (*ghafr*) preceded the actual commission of the sin (*sabaqat al maghfira wuqū' al-dhanb*) [42]. Once it is understood that *ghafr* signifies, etymologically, the "veil" (*sitr*), two possibilities can be seen: either this veil comes between the commission of the sin and the one benefiting from the *ghafr*, in which case no sin of any sort can be committed, or the veil gets placed between the one sinning and the divine punishment that normally ought to be meted out for the sins perpetrated [43]. The former case is obviously referring to the Prophet himself, who is therefore absolutely, and literally, *ma'sūm* ("impeccable") [44].

The second case in this particular scenario refers to certain *awliyā'*, and surely also to the *ahl al-bayt*. Ibn Arabī refers several times in the *Futūhāt* to the somewhat peculiar (to say the least) status of the *awliyā'* [45]. He backs his views with two hadiths, one of which concerns what the Prophet asserted about those who fought at Badr: "What do you know about them? It may be that God looked upon the People of Badr and declared: 'Do as you wish, for I have [already and henceforth] pardoned you'" [46]. The second [47], to which he refers more often, involves the specific case of a servant who immediately asks for God's pardon every time he commits a sin. The third time this happens, God says: "My servant has sinned and he knew he had a Lord who pardons sin and sanctions it. Do as you wish, for I have [already and henceforth] pardoned you! (*i'mal mā shi'ta faqad ghafartu laka*)." For Ibn Arabī, this latter declaration is saying that, as far as the believer is concerned – provided he understands these divine words as being addressed to him specifically [48] – any form of *tahjīr*, anything "forbidden," is suspended. In his case, the only domain operative is that of the *mubāh*, that which is "licit." Ibn Arabī thus compares suspension of *tahjīr* to what happened with Abraham when he was thrown into the fire [49] without getting burned [50]. The norm governing fire, which generally implies something getting burned, was in this case suspended. In just the same way, when these spiritual seekers commit sins, they give the appearance (*sūra*) of doing so, but are removed – from the divine perspective, *and only the divine perspective* – from the state of sin; whence the absence of divine punishment. In other words, these *awliyā'* continue to be subject to legal penalties in this world [51].

The same is true for the *ahl al-bayt*, it might be said. Since sin is the worst of all possible stains, and to the extent that verse 33 of Sura *al-Ahzāb* guarantees the indefectible purity of the *ahl al-bayt*, it necessarily follows, Ibn Arabī says, that they should enjoy the divine absolution so solemnly proclaimed in the second verse of Sura *al-Fath*, just as the Prophet does. This is precisely where their essential purity comes from: in light of the pardon irrevocably granted by God which absolves them *in advance* of any sin, they are *mutahharūn*, "purified" [52]. In other words, the impeccability they enjoy does not in any way mean, in contrast to the Prophet, that they are incapable of committing sins; for them, it is rather a case of God not considering them as being in the state of "sin" (*dhanb*), and they are consequently exempt from divine punishment [53]. Ibn Arabī further makes clear that this pardon will be in effect only in the hereafter, and that the *ahl al-bayt* are indeed subject to legal sanctions when they break the Law [54].

Given the above, it behooves every Muslim, Ibn Arabī emphasizes, to believe steadfastly that God has already and henceforth pardoned the *ahl al-bayt* for any sins they might commit; consequently, one should refrain from blaming any of the "People of the House" in any way, even should one feel he is a victim of their actions [55]. "If you truly loved God and His Messenger," he says in this regard, "you would love the 'People of the [Messenger's] House.' Everything emanating from them that runs counter to your nature or your wishes when it reaches you, you would find beautiful, and you would rejoice upon its arrival" [56].

A final question concerns who the *ahl al-bayt* are, specifically. Here again, Ibn Arabī's answer is unequivocal: it refers to the *shurafā'*, on the one hand, that is, to Fātima's decendants; and on the other, to those who, like Salmān, are connected to the *ahl al-*

bayt and, because of this connection, likewise enjoy the divine absolution promised in the second verse of Sura *al-Fath* [57].

"SALMAN IS ONE OF US..."

Granted, the above still fails to clarify either Salmān's specific status or the nature of the secret regarding where the honor of his being connected to the Prophet's family comes from. For the most part, the relevant details are found at the beginning and at the end of the same chapter 29, although they are not completely understandable unless they are tied together with other passages from the *Futūhāt* where Ibn Arabī discusses Salmān.

The earliest lines of this chapter address the theme of "pure servitude," as mentioned earlier. At the outset, Ibn Arabī cites two supporting hadiths, one after the other. The first of these concerns the *mawālī*s, the "freed slaves" [58]: "One freed by a family is a member of that family (*mawlā al-qawm minhum*)" [59]. According to an account by Ibn Ishāq, Salmān was a slave in Medina at the time of his conversion to Islam, and was freed through the Prophet's intervention when Muhammad organized the conditions for his being bought back. Given this, he gained the status of the Prophet's *mawlā*, thus becoming a de facto member of the *ahl al-bayt*.

The "secret" behind his privileged relationship with the Prophet was nevertheless not the result of his social or legal situation – one which he in fact shared with numerous other *mawālī*s [60]; it was rather due to his sanctity. The second hadith Ibn Arabī uses in his introductory paragraph shines additional light on this: "The men of the Qur'an are men of God and His elite (*Ahlu l-qur'ān hum ahlu Llāh wa khāssatuhu*)" [61]. If we look back at the beginning of chapter 73 in the *Futūhāt*, where the author lists the different categories of saints, we see that one of these categories fits the wording of this hadith precisely [62], as Ibn Arabī mentions those "whose nature is the Qur'an." This is, once again, a reference to the highest degree of spiritual perfection – that, first and foremost, of the Prophet (it was his wife A'isha, as we remember, who declared "His nature was the Qur'an"), and that, secondly, of those on the spiritual path who, once they have reached the peak of *ittibā' al-nabī*, have taken on his spiritual states: "He whose nature is the Qur'an," he says elsewhere in this regard, "brings the Prophet back from the tomb" [63]. It is moreover noteworthy that in chapter 29 Ibn Arabī fleshes out this hadith by telling about his own "absolute servitude," as a kind of label marking the height of sanctity.

The saints in question, whom Ibn Arabī most often calls "Muhammadans," are thus the Prophet's authentic heirs. The relationship is of two different natures, as he explained elsewhere [64].

> The flesh relationship [*qarābat al-tīn*] and the spiritual relationship [*qarābat al-dīn*]; he who combines both forms of relatedness is he whose relationship ties are the most perfect. In the case where one of the two [heirs] has [only] a spiritual connection and the other [only] a connection by blood, the spiritual connection is preeminent. This is what God decided in regard to inheritance: when the heirs are of different religions, the spiritual connection prevails over the fleshly connection. In the case of two brothers, where one is a monotheist [literally: "believing in God alone"] and the other is not [literally: "denying divine oneness"] [65], if one of them dies the other cannot inherit from the first, for the Prophet has stated: "People belonging to two different Traditions [*ahlu millatayn*] do not transfer heritage from one to the other" [66]. Thus when the Prophet's uncle, Abū Ṭālib died, ʿAqīl [who was a polytheist] got his father's property, to the detriment of ʿAlī [67].

This brings us to Salmān's particular case. Ibn Arabī asserts that Salmān had received the spiritual heritage of the Poles who reached the highest state of "spiritual solitude" [68]. This passage's mention of Khadir – who played an eminent role in the initiatory hierarchy, such as Ibn Arabī saw it [69] – as being one of these Poles is also noteworthy [70]. What it means is that Ibn Arabī was thinking especially about the *Malāmiyya* here – the most perfect of the gnostics, sometimes known as the "men of blame" [71] – who, in his hagiology, are the "Muhammadan saints" par excellence. Two other *Futūhāt* texts provide pertinent details. One is the passage at the end of chapter 309 – a chapter entirely devoted to the *Malāmiyya* – where Ibn Arabī states: "The *Malāmiyya* are a supreme category [of saints]; they are the masters of the Ideal Way. [...] Salmān al-Fārisī was one of the most eminent among them, as well as one of the Companions of the Prophet in that station that is the divine station in this world" [72]. We also have a long passage from chapter 14 that deals with the "station of general prophecy" – which is, as we have seen, the highest station that saints can reach. In it, Ibn

Arabī points out that those on the spiritual path who do reach this station are those who preserve both the "spiritual states" (ahwāl) of the Prophet and his knowledge, and he mentions Salmān as one of those from the time of the Prophet who reached this spiritual abode [73].

We thus have three specific and mutually complementary indications of Salmān's spiritual status, since each of them expresses the idea that this illustrious Companion of the Prophet was, in his time, a far from ordinary saint. More specifically, he belonged to the category of Malāmiyya who were, in the Shaykh al-Akbar's eyes, the most highly advanced of the saints in that they adhered fully and in every way possible to the model of spiritual perfection pertinent to the Prophet's specific heritage. Salmān had, moreover, reached the "station of proximity," which is something allowed only to a limited number of Malāmiyya – those who fully embodied "pure servitude," whom Ibn Arabī called the afrād, the "solitary ones" [74].

At this point let us remember that for Ibn Arabī, the term ahl al-bayt refers to two different things. On the one hand, it goes without saying that it applies to the Prophet's family, in the way that word is usually understood – that is, the "People of the Cloak" – and it applies to the shurafāʾ, the "descendants of Fāṭima." The blood ties that join them to the Prophet rightfully guarantee them a certain kind of impeccability, since they will be brought back from death maghfūran lahum, "pardoned," and thus exempt from any divine punishment. Their place on the Prophet's genealogical tree further implies the unfailing veneration of believers and – Ibn Arabī is insistent on this point – this means veneration for every single member of that tree. The Prophet's family comprises a unit unto itself; the love shown to its members, which is their due, cannot be partial [75].

However, beyond descendants linked by blood, there are also descendants linked in spirit. And let it be understood that an individual may, in this case, fit both categories. Like Tirmidhī, Ibn Arabī was of the opinion that Muhammad's spiritual children also belonged to the "House of the Prophet." He frequently used the generic term "Muhammadans" in reference to them, each of whom was characterized by the fact that he had fully, and in every way, actualized the "pure servitude" that characterized the Prophet's spiritual attitude and his relationship with God.

It was this sense of "spiritual posterity" that he had in mind in the long passage from the *Futūhāt*'s chapter 73, where he (somewhat discursively in this case) responded to Tirmidhī's famous question about the meaning of the hadith *Ahlu baytī amān li ummatī* [76]. After asserting once again that "servitude" was the Prophet's essential attribute (*sifatuhu*), he stated: "The 'People of the House' are those who possess the same attribute [pure servitude] as he" [77].

And it is these exceptional beings, whose renunciation perpetuates the "excellent model" [78] incarnated by the Prophet during his life, who are the guardians of his *umma*, his "Community." They protect it from the greatest of all perils, that of eternal damnation. The focus of Ibn Arabī's attention here is on the soteriological role that the tribe of Muhammadan saints will play in the life hereafter, after the Final Judgment has taken place.

In an earlier chapter, Ibn Arabī's teaching regarding universal salvation and its scriptural foundations were discussed somewhat at length. He addressed the issue in several of his writings. To his mind, the issue was a divisive one, and even if the consensus of all was on some form of felicity (either short term, or long term) for all mankind without exception, the arguments at base are nothing less than repetitive. The essential idea common to all is that God's mercy will prevail over His just wrath. All the texts look at the final triumph of *rahma*, "divine mercy," taking place, but from different perspectives. The triumph always unfolds according to the way a certain Qur'anic verse or, as is the case here, a certain hadith suggests; Ibn Arabī reflects deeply on it before reaching his certitude that "God will be merciful to all" [79].

In the case of the hadith *Ahlu baytī amān li ummatī*, the interpretation is a happy prediction: He proclaims: "Consider, then, the divine mercy accorded to Muhammad's *umma* that is contained within these words!" [80]. He then points out that, just as God protected the honor of the "House of the Prophet" in this world by imposing strict rules of conduct upon his wives, so also will He see to safeguarding this honor in the world hereafter, by not permitting a single member of his *umma* to suffer divine punishment eternally: "and this, *because of the blessing upon the ahl al-bayt.*" It happens that Ibn Arabī says this with great frequency, repeating it one more time in this passage: the Prophet's "Community" is, from a certain point of view, all of humanity, in so far as the Prophet was sent to "all of mankind" [81], as Revelation proclaimed. He carried out his mandate behind the scenes at the beginning, via the prophets who preceded him and were his "substitutes" (nuwwāb), and more manifestly later, starting from the moment of his life among men. "Muhammad's umma thus stretches from Adam up to the last man who will exist; from this perspective, everyone is included in Muhammad's Community. All will receive the ahl al-bayt's blessing, and all will enjoy happiness" [82].

In the long Futūhāt chapter he devotes to love, Ibn Arabī asserts that those who love God with complete sincerity get maqtūl, "killed," annihilated [83]. This is what happens to the Muhammadan saints, those who rightfully belong to the "Prophetic House" and walk in the Messenger's footsteps. As "Pure Servants," through their love for God, they have stripped themselves of both their egos and everything else, to the point where they are "without name and without other qualifiers" [84]. This is a voluntary death, offered sacrificially to the "Lord of the Worlds," in exchange for which these "simple, annihilated souls" [85] claim nothing, but by virtue of which God commits to pour the "blood price" (al-diya) over them: the promise that, in recognition of their exemplary sanctity, no one will incur divine wrath for eternity.

Notes:

[1] The complete text of this tradition, of which there are a number of variations, says: "The stars are a safeguard for the People of Heaven, and the People of my House are a safeguard for my Community" (TIRMIDHĪ, 1992 [a], "asl," 22, II, p. 101}.

[2] This has not kept a number of Sunni authors from mentioning it without suggesting any doubt about its authenticity, as may be seen in ibid., in TABARĪ, A., 2004, num. 57, or in IBN HAJAR AL-HAYTAMĪ, 2003, p. 261, num. 12.

[3] TABARĪ, A., 2004, ch. 5; IBN HAJAR AL-HAYTAMĪ, 2003, pp. 260ff.

[4] EI2, "Ahl al-bayt"; AMIR-MOEZZI, 2000; SHARON, 1986.

[5] Qur'an 11:73, 33:33.

[6] TABARĪ, n.d., X, 22nd part, pp. 5-7.

[7] Regarding this event, cf. EI2, "Mubāhala"; MASSIGNON, 1969, I, pp. 550-572.

[8] IBN KATHĪR, 1999, IV, pp. 220-221.

[9] See above, ch. 4, pp. 57ff.

[10] TIRMIDHĪ, 1992 (a), II, pp. 103-108, "asl", 222. Tirmidhī accepts, without any reticence, the authenticity of this statement attributed to the Prophet, while he does judge this other tradition about the ahl al-bayt's preeminence as suspect: Innī tārikun fīkum al-thaqalayn, kitābu Llāh wa 'atratī. The hadith does appear in the canonical collections (WENSINCK, 1936-1969, I, p. 271). In a passage in the appendix, Tirmidhī remarks that the tradition came from the

"People of Kūfa," who in his opinion were scarcely worthy of confidence in issues relating to the chain of transmission, due to their sympathy for the Shi'ites. Even in admitting that it might be authentic, the tradition, he says, only means that believers should respect the rights of the "People of the House" (in the usual sense of the term), and not that they have any particular authority (TIRMIDHĪ, 2002, pp. 93-98). Tirmidhī also discusses this hadith without addressing the issue of its authenticity, but stresses that one should not conclude from it that the *ahl al-bayt* benefited from '*isma*, the "impeccability" that was the exclusive prerogative of the prophets (ID., 1992 [a], I, pp. 163-164, "*asl*", 50 *Nawādir*).

[11] *Ibid.*, II, p. 103; ID., 1965, pp. 344-346; ID., 1992 (b), pp. 44-45. Cf. also RADTKE & O'KANE, 1996, pp. 109, 111.
[12] The *Nawādir* were first published in 1293 A.H. in Istanbul.
[13] NABHANĪ, 1911, pp. 332-333, offers a detailed summary of this event in an appendix titled *Asbāb al-ta'līf*.
[14] Nabhanī cites the *Futūhāt* often, though this does not mean that we can be assured he always understood them (CHODKIEWICZ, 2000).
[15] TIRMIDHĪ, 1965, pp. 344-346; RADTKE & O'KANE, 1996, pp. 109, 111.
[16] CHODKIEWICZ, 1994 (a), pp. 24-25.
[17] IBN ARABĪ, 1911, I, pp. 545-546.
[18] *Ibid.*
[19] This wording is known as the *tasliya ibrāhīmiyya*; it is found in most of the canonical collections (WENSINCK, 1936-1969, III, p. 282).
[20] Let it be understood, Ibn Arabī emphasizes, that the Prophet made this recommendation after a divine revelation and with certainty that this request made by believers would be granted.
[21] Qur'an 33:40.
[22] WENSINCK, 1936-1969, II, p. 260; cf. above, pp. 48ff.
[23] On this theme, cf. CHODKIEWICZ, 1986, pp. 77, 175-176.
[24] Ibn Arabī's remark in regard to these words was that "effort to interpret the Law" (*ijtihād*) is the part of lawgiving prophecy (*nubuwwat al-tashri'*) reserved for the '*ārifūn*. If the latter happen to belong to the family of the Prophet, they bring together in their efforts not only the status of the *āl Muhammad* but also that of the *ahl al-bayt*, as was the case for Hasan and Husayn.
[25] IBN MANZŪR, n.d., vol. XI, pp. 37-39, s.v. "*āl*."
[26] See above, ch. 4, pp. 57ff.
[27] IBN ARABĪ, 1911, II, pp. 127-128; ID., 1972-1992, XIII, pp. 153ff (italics mine).
[28] On this subject, see Ibn Arabī's interpretation of verse 39 in Sura al-Nūr, in IBN ARABĪ, 1911, I, p. 193, II, pp. 269, 338, and the quite enlightening remarks by CHODKIEWICZ, 2001, p. 26, and ID., 1993, pp. 40-41, and p. 144, note 18.
[29] IBN ARABĪ, 1911, IV, pp. 184, 203.
[30] On this theme, see above, ch. 7, pp. 99-100; JĪLĪ, 2004, p. 104.
[31] IBN ARABĪ, 1965, p. 320. At issue is question 150, which thus immediately precedes the question about the expression *āl Muhammad*.
[32] This tradition, which does not appear in the canonical collections, is cited especially by Ibn Ishāq, in IBN HISHĀM, 2001, p. 392. On the different recen-

sions of the hadith, cf. MASSIGNON, 1969, I, "Salmān Pak," pp. 453-454.

[33] On the peculiar fate of Salmān, cf. IBN HISHĀM, 2001, pp. 86ff; MASSIGNON, 1969, I, pp. 443-483; EI2, "Salmān."

[34] IBN ARABĪ, 1911, I, pp. 195-199; ID., 1972-1992, III, pp. 227-242.

[35] ID., 1911, II, pp. 13, 263, IV, p. 62.

[36] On the idea of "pure servitude," cf. CHODKIEWICZ, 1994 (a), pp. 121-129.

[37] IBN ARABĪ, 1971-1992, III, pp. 229-230.

[38] Ibid., p. 230.

[39] Ibid.

[40] IBN ARABĪ, 1911, I, p. 622, II, p. 359, IV, pp. 145, 490.

[41] See above, ch. 3, p. 52-53.

[42] Ibid., I, p. 622, II, p. 359.

[43] Ibid., I, p. 622, III, pp. 178-179.

[44] ID., 1965, question 157, p. 325.

[45] ID., 1911, I, pp. 622, 661, II, pp. 491, 512-513, 553, III, p. 563, IV, pp. 49, 145, 162.

[46] MUSLIM, n.d., IV, p. 1941, "fadā'il al-sahaba," 161; GRAHAM, 1977, p. 120.

[47] MUSLIM, n.d., IV, p. 2112, "tawba," 29; GRAMAH, 1977, p. 119.

[48] IBN ARABĪ, 1911, II, p. 512.

[49] Qur'an 21:69.

[50] IBN ARABĪ, 1911, I, p. 233.

[51] Note that Ibn Arabī indicated – in his k. al-Mubashshirāt, or "Book of Visions," (IBN ARABĪ, ms., folio 92) – he heard God pronounce, to him, the famous words "Do what you wish!" (i'mal mā shi'ta...).

[52] ID., 1972-1992, III, pp. 230-231.

[53] Ibid., I, p. 622, II, p. 513.

[54] ID., 1972-1992, III, p. 231.

[55] Ibid., pp. 234ff.

[56] Ibid., p. 238. Here I am summarizing, in just a few lines, several long passages that Ibn Arabī dedicates to the duty of veneration for the ahl al-bayt, an indication of the importance he accords to the practice.

[57] Ibid., pp. 230-231.

[58] On the different meanings of the word mawlā, cf. EI2, "mawlā."

[59] WENSINCK, 1936-1969, VII, p. 333.

[60] See the list of the Prophet's mawālīs as drawn up, for example, by TABARĪ, 1980, p. 331.

[61] WENSINCK, 1936-1969, V, p. 346.

[62] IBN ARABĪ, 1911, II, p. 20.

[63] Ibid., IV, p. 61.

[64] Ibid., III, p. 532; cf. also ibid., p. 168; ID., 2010, pp. 191, 249, 257.

[65] It is interesting to note that, at two different points in this passage, the example Ibn Arabī offers is not that of two brothers with different beliefs properly speaking, but only the case where one of the two is actually an idolater. This suggests an interpretation of the hadith relative to the inheritance cited in the passage that is not limited to its legal definition.

[66] WENSINCK, 1936-1969, VII, p. 186.

[67] Let it be remembered that 'Alī and 'Aqīl were both sons of Abū Tālib, but while

the former converted to Islam early on in the Prophet's preaching, ʿAqīl did not renounce his paganism until much later. Abū Ṭālib himself did not make a profession of faith before his death, and thus it was ʿAqīl who received the inheritance.

[68] IBN ARABĪ, 1972-1992, III, p. 233.

[69] CHODKIEWICZ, 1986, pp. 120ff.

[70] IBN ARABĪ, 1972-1992, III, p. 239.

[71] Understanding all the implications of the often allusive remarks made in this chapter on Salmān's spiritual status implies a depth of knowledge regarding Ibn Arabī' hagiology, and especially his teachings about the *Malāmiyya* (cf. the in-depth study by CHODKIEWICZ, 1998, pp. 15-27).

[72] IBN ARABĪ, 1911, III, p. 36.

[73] *Ibid.*, I, p. 151.

[74] IBN ARABĪ, 1972-1992, III, p. 233, states that spiritual seekers who have fully realized "pure servitude" and who consequently are attached to God Himself (Qurʾan 15:42: "You have no power over *My* servants [*ʿibādī*]!") are superior to those who are attached to created beings, *even if the latter are related to the Prophet by blood.*

[75] ID., 1911, IV, p. 139.

[76] *Ibid.*, II, pp. 126-127.

[77] *Ibid.*, p. 126. Ibn Arabī here once again cited from the outset the hadith *Ahlu l-quʾrān...*and the one about Salmān (*Salmān minnā...*) to help delineate what he meant in this particular use of the expression *ahl al-bayt.*

[78] Qurʾan 33:21.

[79] IBN ARABĪ, 1911, II, p. 220.

[80] *Ibid.*, p. 126.

[81] Qurʾan 34:28.

[82] IBN ARABĪ, 1911, II, p. 127.

[83] *Ibid.*, pp. 350, 354.

[84] *Ibid.*, IV, p. 13.

[85] This expression comes from the title of the beautiful work by PORETE, 1984: *Le miroir des âmes simples et anéanties.*

Acknowledgments

This book is the culmination of several years of research during which I have often called upon the assistance of colleagues and friends. All rose to the task. To them I extend my gratitude for their patient generosity.

I must also acknowledge my debt to my family, and in particular to my father and my husband: without their enduring support this work would never have seen the light of day.

Bibliography

'Abd al-Qādir al-Jazā'irī, *Kitāb al-mawāqif*, Damascus, 1966, 3 vols.

———, *Ecrits spirituels*, trans. M. Chodkiewicz, Paris, 1982.

———, *Le Livre des Haltes*, trans. M. Lagarde, Leiden, 2000, 3 vols.

Abdel-Kader, A. H., *The Life, Personality and Writings of Al-Junayd*, London, 1962.

'Abdī Efendī al-Busnāwī, *Matāli' al-nūr al-saniyy*, IFAO, Cairo, 2013.

Abū Dāwūd, *Sunan*, Beirut, Mecca, 1998, 5 vols.

Abū Nu'aym, *Hilyat al-awliyā'*, Beirut, 1967, 10 vols.

Addas, C., "Expérience et doctrine de l'amour chez Ibn Arabī" in *Mystique musulmane, parcours en compagnie d'un chercheur: Roger Deladrière*, Paris, 2002, pp. 125-139.

———, *Ibn Arabī ou la Quête du Soufre Rouge*, Paris, 1989.

'Ajlūnī, I. (al-), *Kashf al-khafā' wa muzīl al-ilbās*, Beirut, 1351 A.H.

Amir-Moezzi, M., *The Divine Guide in Early Shi'ism: The Sources of Esotericism in Islam,* Albany, New York: State University of New York Press, 1994.

———, "Considérations sur l'expression '*dīn 'Alī*': aux origines de la foi shi'ite," in *Zeitschrift der Deutschen Morgenländischen Gesellschaft*, 150/1, Mainz, 2000, pp. 29-68.

Andrae, T., *Die Person Muhammeds in Lehre und Glauben seiner Gemeinde*, Stockholm, 1918.

Arabic Literature of Africa, vol. 1: "The Writings of Eastern Sudanic Africa to c. 1900," ed. R. S. O'Fahey, Leiden, 1994.

Ashkal, M. (al-), *al-'Itr al-wardī fī karamāt wa mubashshirāt wa 'ulūm al-shaykh Ismā'īl al-Jabartī*, Beirut, 2008.

Atlagh, R., *Contribution à l'étude de la pensée mystique d'Ibn Arabī et son école à travers l'œuvre de 'Abd al-Karīm al-Jīlī*, thèse de doctorat, EPHE, 2000.

Awn P., *Satan's Tragedy and Redemption: Iblīs in Sufi Psychology*, Leiden, 1983.

'Ayn al-Qudāt Hamādhānī, *Tamhīdāt*, trans. C. Tortel, *Les tentations métaphysiques*, Paris, 1992.

'Ayyāshi, A. S. (al-), *al-Rihlat al-'ayyāshiyya*, Abu Dhabi, 2006, 2 vols.

Baghdādī, I. (al-), *Hadiyyat al-'ārifīn*, Istanbul, 1951, 2 vols.

Balī Efendī, *Sharh fusūs al-hikam*, Istanbul, 1309 A.H.

Ballanfat, P., "La prophétologie dans le *'Ayn al-hayāt, tafsīr* attribué à Najm al-Dīn Kubrā", in *Mystique musulmane, parcours en compagnie d'un chercheur: Roger Deladrière*, Paris, 2002, pp. 171-364.

Baqlī Ruzbehān, *Sharh-i shathiyāt*, ed., Corbin, Paris 1966.

Bar-Asher, M., *Scripture and Exegesis in Early Imāmī Shiism*, Leiden, 1999.

Bidlīsī, 'A. (al-), *Bahjat al-tā'ifa wa sawm al-qalb*, ed. E. Badeen, Beirut, 1999.

———, *Sawm al-qalb*, in *ibid.*

Böwering, G., *The Mystical Vision of Existence in Classical Islam,* Berlin-New York, 1980.

Brenner, L., "Sufism in Africa in the Seventeenth and Eighteenth Centuries" in *Islam et sociétés au sud du Sahara*, num. 2, Paris, 1988, pp. 80-93.

Brockelmann, (C.) *Geschichte der Arabischen Literatur*, Leiden, 1937-1949.

Bukhārī, M. (al-), *Sahīh*, ed. M. al-Nāsir, Beirut, 1422 A.H., 4 vols.

Burhānī, 'U. (al-), *Tabri'at al-dhimma*, s.l.n.d., Beirut, 2010.

Chih, R., "Les débuts d'une *tarīqa*. Formation et essor de la Halwatiyya égyptienne au XVIIIe siècle d'après l'hagiographie de son fondateur, Muhammad ibn Sālim al-Hifnī (d. 1181/1767) in *Le Saint et son milieu*, IFAO, Cairo, 2000, pp.137-149.

———, and Mayeur-Jaouen, C., *Le Soufisme à l'époque ottomane*, IFAO, Cairo, 2010, Introduction, pp. 1-57.

Chittick, W. C., "The Origin of Creation," in *Les Illuminations de La Mecque*, Paris, 1989, pp. 77-93.

Chodkiewicz, M., *Le Sceau des saints. Prophétie et sainteté dans la doctrine d'Ibn Arabī*, Paris, 1986; revised and expanded edition, Paris, 2012. (English trans. *Seal of the Saints: Prophethood and Sainthood in the Doctrine of Ibn Arabi*, Cambridge, 1993).

———, *Un océan sans rivage. Ibn Arabī, le Livre et Loi*, Paris, 1992.

———, *An Ocean without a Shore: Ibn Arabi, The Book and the Law*, Albany, New York: State University of New York Press, 1994.

———, "Le modèle prophétique de la sainteté en Islam," *al-Masaq, studia arabo-islámica mediterranea*, vol. VII, Leeds, 1994, pp. 201-226.

———, "The Banner of Praise," in *The Journal of the Muhyiddin Ibn 'Arabi Society,* vol. XXI, *Praise*, Oxford, 1997, pp. 45-58.

———, "Les Malāmiyya dans la doctrine d'Ibn Arabī," in *Melāmis-Bayrāmis. Études sur trois mouvements mystiques musulmans*, Istanbul, 1998, pp. 15-25.

———, "Le procès posthume d'Ibn Arabī," in *Islamic Mysticism Contested. Thirteen Centuries of Controversies and Polemics*, ed. F. De Jong and B. Radtke, Leiden, 1999, pp. 93-123.

———, "La somme des miracles des saints de Nabhānī," in *Miracles et karāma*, Turnhout, 2000, pp. 607-622.

———, "Maître Eckhart et Ibn Arabī," in *Mémoire dominicaine*, Paris, 2001, num. 15, pp. 21-35.

———, "Les trois cailloux du shaykh 'Abd al-Karīm al-Jīlī," in *Mystique musulmane. Parcours en compagnie d'un chercheur: Roger Deladrière*, Paris, 2002, pp. 142-154.

———, "Shaykh Muhammad Demirdāsh: un soufi akbarien au XVIᵉ siècle," in *Horizons maghrébins*, num. 51, 2004, Toulouse, pp. 20-28.

———, "Le paradoxe de la Ka'ba," in *Revue de l'histoire des religions*, vol. XXII, fasc. 4, Paris, 2005, pp. 436-461.

———, "La réception de la doctrine d'Ibn Arabī dans le monde ottoman," in *Sufism and Sufis in Ottoman Society. Sources, Doctrine, Rituals, Turuq, Architecture, Literature, Iconography, Modernism*, Ankara, 2005, pp. 97-120.

———, "*Mi'rāj al-kalima*: de la *Risāla qushayriyya aux Futūhāt makkiyya*," in *Reason and Inspiration in Islam*, ed. T. Lawson, London, 2005, pp. 248-262.

Cirillo, L., "Verus Propheta," in *Henri Corbin*, Cahier de l'Herne, C. Jambet (dir.), num. 39, 1981, pp. 240-255.

Corbin, H., *En Islam Iranien*, 4 vols., Paris, 1991.

Cornell, V., "Mystical Doctrine and Political Action in Morrocan Sufism: the Role of the Exemplar in the Tarīqa jazūliyya," in *Al-Qantara*, vol. XIII, fasc. I, Madrid, 1992, pp. 205-237.

Daylamī, *Kitab 'Atf al-alif*, ed. J.-C. Vadet, Cairo, 1962.

Drewes, G. W. J., "A Note on Muhammad al-Sammān, His Writings, and 19th Century Sammāniyya Practices, Chiefly in Batavia, According to Written Data," in *Archipel*, vol. XLIII, Paris, 1992, pp.73-87.

Ebstein, M., Sviri, S., "The So-Called *Risālat al-hurūf* (Epistle on Letters) Ascribed to Sahl al-Tustarī and Letter Mysticism in al-Andalus," *Journal asiatique*, vol. CCXCIX, num. 1, 2011, pp. 213-270.

EI2 (Encyclopedie de l'Islam), 2nd ed., Leiden, 1960-2002, 13 vols.

El Adnani, J., "Les origines de la Tijāniyya: quand les premiers disciples se mettent à parler," in J.-L. Triaud and D. Robinson (ed.), *La Tijāniyya. Une confrérie musulmane à la conquête de l'Afrique*, Karthala, 2005, pp. 35-69.

Elmore, G. T., *Islamic Sainthood in the Fullness of Time. Ibn al-ʿArabī's Book of the Fabulus Gryphon*, Leiden, Boston, Cologne, 1999.

Ernst, C. W., "Muhammad as the Pole of Existence," in *The Cambridge Companion to Muhammad*, ed. J. Brockopp, Cambridge, 2010, pp. 123-138.

Fierro, M., "La polémique à propos de *rafʿ al-yadayn fī l-salāt* dans al-Andalus," *Studia Islamica*, vol. LXV, Paris, 1987, pp. 69-90.

Gaborieau, M., Grandin, N., "Le renouveau confrérique," in A. Popovic and G. Veinstein (dir.). *Les Voies d'Allāh. Les ordres mystiques dans le monde musulman des origines à aujourd'hui*, Paris, 1996, pp. 68-87.

Geoffroy, E., *Le Soufisme en Égypte et en Syrie*, Damascus, 1995.

———, "Le traité de soufisme d'un disciple d'Ibn Taymiyya: Ahmad al-Wāsitī (m. 711/1311)," in *Studia Islamica*, Paris, 1995, num. 82, pp. 83-103.

———, "La voie du blâme: une modalité majeure de la sainteté en islam d'après l'exemple du cheikh ʿAlī b. Maymūn al-Fāsī," in N. Amry and D. Gril (dir.), *Saints et sainteté dans le christianisme et l'islam*, Paris, 2008, pp. 139-151.

Ghazālī, A. H. (al-), *Mishkāt al-anwār*, Cairo, 1964. French ed. *Le Tabernacle des Lumières*, trans. R. Deladrière, Paris, 1981.

Ghazzī, N. (al-), *al-Kawākib al-sāʾira bi aʿyān al-miʾa al-ʿāshira*, Beirut, 1997, 3 vols.

Gobillot, G., *Le Livre de la profondeur des choses*, Lille, 1996.

———, *La Conception originelle, ses interprétations et fonctions chez les penseurs musulmans*, IFAO, Cairo, 2000.

———, "'Fatara' et 'fitra,' quelques acceptions oubliées," in *En hommage au père Jacques Jomier, O.P.*, Paris, 2002, pp.101-121.

———, "Le *Mahdī*, le *Khatm al-awliyāʾ* et le *Qutb*," in *Mélanges de Science Religieuse*, Université Catholique de Lille, num. 59, 2002, pp. 5-30.

Goldziher, I., *Études sur la tradition islamique extraites du tome II des "Muhammedanische Studien*," trans. L. Bercher, Paris, 1984.

Graham, W. A., *Divine Word and Prophetic Word in Early Islam*, The Hague, 1977.

Gril, D., "La science des lettres," in *Les Illuminations de La Mecque*, Paris, 1989, pp. 385-486.

———, "Le ḥadīth dans l'œuvre d'Ibn Arabī ou la chaîne ininterrompue de la prophétie," in *Das Prophetenhadīt. Dimensionen einer islamischen Literaturgattung*, ed. C. Gilliot and T. Nagel, Göttingen, 2005, pp. 123-144.

———, "De la *khirqa* à la *tarīqa*: continuité et évolution dans l'identification et la classification des voies," in *Le Soufisme à l'époque ottomane*, IFAO, Cairo, 2010, pp. 57-81.

Ḥājjī Khalīfa, *Kashf al-zunūn ʿan asāmī al-kutub wa-l-funūn*, Beirut, n.d., 2 vols.

Ḥakīm, S. (al-), *al-Muʿjam al-ṣūfī*, Beirut, 1981.

Hallāj, H., *Kitāb al-tawāsīn*, ed. L. Massignon, Paris, 1913.

Ḥaqqī, I., *Tafsīr rūh al-bayān*, n.d., n.p., 10 vols.

Ḥawwāt, S. (al-), *al-Rawda al-maqsūda wa l-hulal al-mamdūda fī maʾāthir banī sūda*, Fès, 1994, 2 vols.

Hoffman, V., "Devotion to the Prophet and his Family in Egyptian Sufism," in *Middle East Studies*, vol. XXIV, 1992, pp. 615-637.

———, *Sufism, Mystics and Saints in Modern Egypt*, University of South Carolina, 1995.

- "Annihilation in the Messenger of God: The Development of a Sufi Practice," in *International Journal of Middle East Studies*, vol. XXXI, Cambridge, 1999, pp. 351-369.

Ibn al-Ahdal, *Kashf al-ghitāʾ ʿan haqāʾiq al-tawhīd wa l-radd ʿalā Ibn Arabī al-faylasūf al-ṣūfī*, Tunis, 1964.

Ibn ʿAjība, *Deux Traités sur l'Unité de l'Existence*, trans. and presented by J.-L. Michon, Marrakech, 1998.

Ibn ʿAlawī (m. al-Mālikī), *al-Dhakhāʾir al-muhammadiyya*, Cairo, n.d.

Ibn ʿArabī, *K. ʿAnqā al-mughrib fī maʿrifati khatm al-awliyāʾ*, Cairo, 1954.

———, *Al-Ajwiba al-ʿarabiyya fī sharh al-masāʾil al-yūsufiyya*, Beirut, 2010.

———, *K. al-Bulghat al-ghawwās fī l-akwān*, ed. Mizyadī, Beirut, 2011.

———, *al-Dawr al-aʿlā (Hizb al-wiqāya). A Prayer for Spiritual Elevation*, critical edition and translation by Suha Taji-Farouki, Oxford, 2006.

———, *K. al-Fanāʾ*, in *Rasāʾil ibn al-Arabī*, Hyderabad, 1948.

———, *al-Futūhāt al-makkiyya*, Cairo, 1911 (1329 A.H.), 4 vols.; critical edition by O. Yahia, Cairo, 1972-1992, 14 vols.

———, *Fusūs al-hikam*, ed. Afīfī, Beirut, 1980.

———, *K. al-Hujub*, in *Majmū' al-rasā'il al-ilāhiyya*, Beirut, 1991.

———, *K. al-Isrā'*, ed. S. Hakīm, Beirut, 1988.

———, *al-Jawāb al-mustaqīm*, in Tirmidhī, *Kitāb Khatm al-awliyā'*, ed. O. Yahia, Beirut, 1965.

———, *K. al-Kunh*, Cairo, 1967.

———, *Majmū'at al-ahzāb*, Istanbul, n.d.

———, *K. Manzil al-qutb*, Hyderabad, 1948.

———, *K. al-Mubashshirāt*, ms. Fātih, 5322, ff. 90-93.

———, *Muhādarāt al-abrār wa musāmarāt al-akhyār*, Cairo, 1906, 2 vols.

———, *Rūh al-quds*, Damascus, 1970.

———, *K. al-Tarājim*, in *Rasā'il ibn al-Arabī*, Hyderabad, 1948.

———, *K. 'Uqlat al-mustawfiz*, in *Kleinere Schriften des Ibn al-'Arabī*, ed. H.S. Nyberg, Leiden, 1919, pp. 49-99.

———, *La profession de foi*, trans. R. Deladrière, Paris, 1978.

Ibn 'Atā' Allāh al-Iskandarī, *Latā'if al-minan*, Damascus, 1992; French trans. *La Sagesse des mâitres sufis*, trans. E. Geoffroy, Paris, 1998.

Ibn Hajar al-'Asqalānī, *Inbā' al-ghumr bi anbā' al-'umr*, Cairo 1968-1972, 4 vols.

Ibn Hajar al-Haytamī, *al-Sawā'iq al-muhriqa fī l-radd 'alā ahl al-bida' wa l-zindiqa*, Istanbul, 2003.

Ibn Hanbal, *Musnad*, Beirut, 1995-2001, 50 vols.

Ibn Hishām, *al-Sīra al-nabawiyya*, Beirut, 2001.

Ibn al-'Imād, *Shadharāt al-dhahab fī akhbār man dhahaba*, Beirut, 1979, 8 vols.

Ibn al-Jawzī, *Sifat al-safwa*, Beirut, 1986, 3 vols.

———, *al-Wafā bi ahwāl al-mustafā*, Beirut, 1988.

Ibn Kathīr, *Tafsīr al-qur'ān al-'azīm*, Beirut, 1999, 5 vols.

Ibn al-Khatīb, *Rawd al-ta'rīf*, Beirut, 1970, 2 vols.

Ibn Kīrān, *Sharh al-salāt al-mashīshiyya*, Abū Dhabī, 1999.

Ibn Manzūr, *Lisān al-'arab*, Beirut, n.d., 15 vols.

Ibn Qasī, *Kitāb khal' al-na'layn wa iqtibās al-nūr*, ed. M. Amrānī, Marrakech, 1997.

Ibn Sab'īn, *Rasā'il Ibn Sab'īn*, ed. 'A. R. Badawī, Cairo, 1965.

Ibn Sa'd, *Kitāb al-tabaqāt al-kabīr*, Leiden, 1909, 8 vols.

Ibn Taymiyya, *Majmū'at al-rasā'il wa l-masā'il*, Cairo, n.d, 2 vols.

Isfarāyinī, N. D. (al-), *Le Révélateur des mystères. Traité de soufisme*, ed. and trans. H. Landolt, Verdier, 1986.

'Iyād (al-Qādī), *al-Shifā' bi ta'rīf huqūq al-mustafā*, Beirut, n.d.

Jabartī, 'A. R. (al-), *Ajā'ib al-athār fī l-tarājim wa l-āthār*, Cairo, 1998, 4 vols.

Jandī, M. D. (al-), *Sharh fusūs al-hikam*, Mashhad, 1982.

Jazūlī, M. (al-), *Dalā'il al-khayrāt wa shawāriq al-anwār*, Casablanca, 2011.

Jīlī, 'A. K. (al-), *al-Insān al-kāmil*, Cairo, 1970; excerpts trans. by T. Burckhardt, "De l'Homme Universel. Extraits du livre 'al-Insān al-Kāmil,'" Paris, 1975.

———, *al-Kahf wa l-raqīm*, Hyderabad, 1985; new edition, Beirut, 2015.

———, *al-Kamālāt al-ilāhiyya fī l-sifāt al-muhammadiyya*, Beirut, 2004.

———, *Lawāmi' al-barq al-mūhin*, Beirut, 2010.

———, *Marātib al-wujūd*, Beirut, 2005.

———, *Nasīm al-sahar*, Beirut, 2005.

———, *Qāb qawsayn wa multaqā al-namūsayn*, ms. Esad Efendi, 1665, folios 16-38, in 'Uthmān al-Burhānī, *Tabri'at al-dhimma fī nush al-umma*, n.d., n.p., new edition, Beirut, 2010.

———, *Sharh mushkilāt al-futūhāt al-makkiyya*, Kuwait, 1992.

———, *K. Sirr al-nūr al-munkamin*, ms. Esad Efendi, 1665, folios 39-53.

———, *K. al-Talsam al-mughnī*, ms. Esad Efendi, 1665, folios 172-181b.

———, *Ghunyat arbāb al-samā'*, ms. British Library, India Office Collections, B459B, folios 211-296.

Junayd, A. Q., *Enseignement spirituel*, trans. R. Deladrière, Paris, 1983.

Kalābādhī, A. B. (al-), *Traité de soufisme*, trans. R. Deladrière, Paris, 1981.

Kamāl Ja'far, M., *Min al-turāth al-sūfī. Sahl b. 'Abd Allāh al-Tustarī*, Cairo, 1974.

———, *Min qadāyā al-fikr al-islāmī. Dirāsa wa nusūs*, Cairo, 1978.

Kaptein, N., *Muhammad's Birthday Festival. Early History in the Central Muslim Lands and Development in the Muslim West until the 10th and 16th Century*, Leiden, 1993.

Katz, M.H., *The Birth of the Prophet Muhammad. Devotional Piety in Sunni Islam*, London, 2007.

Khazrajī, 'A. (al-), *al-'Uqūd al-lu'lu'iyya fī ta'rīkh al-dawla al-rasūliyya*, Beirut, 1983, 2 vols.

Knysh, A., *Ibn Arabī in the Later Tradition. The Making of a Polemical Image in Medieval Islam*, New York, 1997.

Kurdī, M. A. (al-) *Tanwīr al-qulūb fī mu'āmalati 'Allām al-ghuyūb*, Beirut, 1995.

Lamatī, A. (al-), *al-Ibrīz min kalām sīdī al-ghawth 'Abd al-'Azīz al-Dabbāgh*, Damascus, 1984, 2 vols.; English trans. *Pure Gold from the Words of Sayyidī 'Abd al-'Aziz al-Dabbāgh*, trans. J. O'Kane, B. Radtke, Leiden-Boston, 2007.

Makdisi, G., "L'islam hanbalisant" in *Revue des études islamiques*, special issue, num. 10, Paris 1983.

Maqqarī, A. (al-), *Nafh al-tīb min ghusn al-andalus al-ratīb*, Beirut, 1986, 11 vols.

Massignon, L., *Essai sur les origines du lexique technique de la mystique musulmane*, Paris, 1968.

―――, *Opera minora*, Paris, 1969, 3 vols.

―――, *La Passion de Hallāj*, Paris, 1975, 4 vols.

McGregor, R. J. A., *Sanctity and Mysticism in Medieval Egypt: The Wafā' Sufī Order and The Legacy of Ibn 'Arabī*, New York, 2004.

―――, "A Fourteenth Century Inheritance of Ibn Arabī's Herme-neutics: the *Nafā'is al-'Irfān* of Muhammad Wafā," in *Symbolisme et hermeneutique dans la pensée d'Ibn Arabī*, coörd. Bakri Aladdin, IFPO, Damascus, 2007, pp. 163-175.

Meier, F., "Invoking Blessings on Muhammad in Prayers of Suppli-cation and When Making Requests," in *Essays on Islamic Piety and Mysticism*, Leiden, 1999, pp. 549-588.

―――, "Poetic Refrain and Mahyā," in *Essays on Islamic Piety and Mysticism*, Leiden, 1999, pp. 649-681.

―――, "A Resurrection of Muhammad in Suyūtī," in *Essays on Islamic Piety and Mysticism*, Leiden, 1999, pp. 505-547.

Memon, M. U., *Ibn Taymiyya's Struggle against Popular Religion,* The Hague-Paris, 1976.

Michon, J. L., *L'Autobiographie du Soufi marocain Ahmad Ibn Ajība*, Milan, 1982.

Munāwī, 'A. R. (al-), *al-Kawākib al-duriyya fī tarājim al-sāda al-sūfiya*, Beirut, 1999, 5 vols.

Muslim, *Sahīh*, Beirut, n.d., 5 vols.

Mustafā Balī Zāde, *Sharh fusūs al-hikam*, Beirut, 2002.

Nabhānī, Y. (al-), *Afdalu al-salawāt alā sayyid al-sadāt*, Beirut, 1996.

———, *Jāmiʿ karamāt al-awliyāʾ*, Beirut, 1983, 2 vols.

———, *Jāmiʿ karamāt al-awliyāʾ*, Cairo, 1911.

———, *Jawāhir al-bihār fī fadāʾil al-nabī al-mukhtār*, Beirut, 1998, 4 vols.

———, *Saʿādat al-dārayn fī l-salāt ʿalā sayyid al-kawnayn*, Beirut, 1997.

———, *Shawāhid al-haqq fī l-istighātha bi sayyid al-khalq*, Beirut, 1996.

Nābulusī, ʿA. G. (al-), *Jawāhir al-nusūs fī hall kalimāt al-fusūs*, Istanbul, 1304 A.H.

Nawwāb, I. (al-), *al-Hadiyya al-rashīdiyya fī l-ijtimāʿ bi sayyid al-bariyya*, ms., University of Riyād, num. 5934, folios 1-49.

Nīsābūrī, H. b. M. (al-), *Tafsīr gharāʾib al-qurʾān wa gharāʾib al-furqān*, ed. in margin of *Jāmiʿ al-bayān* of Tabarī, Beirut, n.d., 12 vols.

Nwyia, P., "Le *tafsīr* mystique attribué à Gaʿfar Sādiq," *Mélanges de l'université Saint-Joseph*, vols. 43, fasc. 4, Beirut, n.d., 12 vols.

———, *Exégèse coranique et langage mystique*, Beirut, 1991.

———, *Trois oeuvres inédites de mystiques musulmans*, Beirut, 1986.

O'Fahey, R. S., *Enigmatic Saint. Ahmad Ibn Idrīs and the Idrisi tradition*, London, 1990.

———, "Pietism, Fundamentalism and Mysticism: An Alternative view of the 18th and 19th century Islamic World," in *Festkrift til Historisk institutts 40-ars jubileum*, 1997, Bergen, pp. 151-166.

———, and Radtke, B., "Neo-Sufism Reconsidered," in *Der Islam*, vol. LXX, num. 1, 1993, pp. 52-87.

Padwick, C., *Muslim Devotion. A Study of Prayer-Manuals in Common Use*, London, 1961.

Pagani, S., "*Défendre le soufisme par des temps difficiles: ʿAbd al-Ghanī al-Nābulusī, polémiste anti-puritain*," in *Le Soufisme à l'époque ottomane*, IFAO, Cairo, 2010, pp. 309-335.

Porete, M., *Le Miroir des âmes simples et anéanties*, Paris, 1984.

Al-Qārī al-Baghdādī, *Manāqib Ibn Arabī*, Beirut, 1959.

Qāshānī, ʿA.R. (al-), *Sharh fusūs al-hikam*, Cairo, 1987.

Qastallānī, A. b. M. (al-), *al-Mawāhib al-laduniyya bi l-minah al-muhammadiyya*, in Zurqānī, *Sharh al-mawāhib*, Beirut, 1996, 12 vols.

Qaysarī, D. (al-), *Sharh fusūs al-hikam*, lithography, Bombay, 1380 A.H.

Qūnāwī, S. D (al-), *Sharh al-arbaʿīn hadīthan*, ed. Hasan Kāmil Yilmaz,

Istanbul, 1990.

Qurtubī, M. b. A. (al-), *al-Jāmiʻ li ahkām al-qur'ān*, Cairo, 1950, 20 parts, 10 vols.

Qushayrī, 'A. K. (al-), *Latā'if al-ishārāt*, Beirut, 2000, 3 vols.

Radtke, B., "Between Projection and Suppression: Some Considerations Concerning the Study of Sufism," in F. De Jong (ed.), *Shi'a Islam, Sects and Sufism*, Utrecht, 1992, pp. 70-82.

———, "Ibrīziana," in *Sudanic Africa*, num. 7, 1996, pp. 113-158.

———, "Sufism in the 18ᵗʰ Century: An Attempt at a Critical Appraisal," in *Die Welt des Islams*, vols. XXXVI, Leiden, 1996, pp. 326-364.

———, "A Reconsideration Reconsidered," in *Neue kritische Gänge. Zu Stand und Aufgaben der Sufikforschung*, Utrecht, 2005, pp. 293-316.

———, O'Fahey, R. S. and O'Kane, J., "Two Sufi Treatises of Ahmad Ibn Idrīs" in *Oriens*, vol. XXXV, Leiden, 1996, pp. 143-178.

———, and O'Kane, J., *The Concept of Sainthood in Early Islamic Mysticism*, Richmond, 1996.

———, O'Kane, J., Vikor, K. S., and O'Fahey, R. S., *The Exoteric Ahmad Ibn Idrīs. A Sufi's Critique of the Madhāhib and the Wahhābīs*, Leiden, 1999.

Rāzī, F. al-D. (al-), *al-tafsīr al-kabīr*, Tehran, n.d, 32 parts, 16 vols.

Rāzī, N. al-D. (al-), *The Path of God's Bondsmen from Origin to Return*, trans. H. Algar, New York, 1982.

Reichmuth, S., *The World of Murtadā al-Zabīd. Life, Networks and Writings*, Oxford, 2009.

———, "Murtadā al-Zabīdī and his Role in 18ᵗʰ Century Sufism," in *Le Soufisme à l'époque ottomane*, IFAO, Cairo, 2010, pp. 383-407.

Répertoire général des oevres d'Ibn Arabī, in *Histoire et classification de l'oeuvre d'Ibn 'Arabī*, Damascus, 1964, 2 vols.

Rubin, U., "Pre-Existence and Light: Aspects of the Concept of *Nūr Muhammad*," in *Israel Oriental Studies*, vol. V, 1975, pp. 62-119.

Ruzbehān Baqlī, *Sharh-i shathiyāt*, ed. H. Corbin, Tehran-Paris, 1966.

Safadī, S. D. (al-), *Aʻyān al-ʻasr wa aʻwān al-ʻasr*, Damascus, 1998, 6 vols.

Sā'in al-Dīn Turkah, *Sharh fusūs al-hikam*, Qom, 1420 A.H.

Sammān, M. (al-), *al-Futūhāt al-ilāhiyya fī l-tawajjuhāt al-rūhiyya li l-hadra al-muhammadiyya*, ms., Cairo, 602, general num. 28934, folios 53-59; Nabhānī, *Jawāhir al-bihār*, IV, Beirut, 1998, pp. 172-180.

Sanūsī, M. (al-), *al-Manhal al-rawī*, Beirut, 1968.

———, *al-Salsabīl al-muʿīn fī l-tarāʾiq al-ʿarbaʿīn*, Beirut, 1968.

Schimmel, A., *And Muhammad is His Messenger: The Veneration of the Prophet in Islamic Piety*, Chapel Hill, 1984.

Sedgwick, M., *Saints and Sons: The Making and Remaking of the Rashīdī Ahmadī Sufi Order 1799-2000*, Leiden-Boston, 2005.

Shaʾrānī, ʿA. W. (al-), *al-Anwār al-qudsiyya fī maʿrifa qawāʾid al-sūfiyya*, Beirut, 1985.

———, *Lawāqih al-anwār al-qudsiyya fī bayān al ʿuhūd al-muhammadiyya*, Aleppo, 1993.

———, *al-Tabaqāt al-kubrā*, Cairo, n.d.

Sharjī, A. (al-), *Tabaqāt al-khawwās ahl al-sidq wa l-ikhlās*, Cairo, 1321 A.H.

Sharon, M., "*Ahl al-Bayt* – People of the House," in *Jerusalem Studies in Arabic and Islam*, num. 8, 1986, pp. 169-184.

Sitt ʿAjam, *Sharh al-mashāhid al-qudsiyya*, ed. B. Aladdin and S. al-Hakim, Damascus, IFPO, 2004.

Subkī, T.D. (al-), *al-Rasāʾil al-subkiyya*, Beirut, 1983.

———, *Shifāʾ al-siqām fī ziyāra khayr al-anām*, extensive excerpts cited in Nabhanī, 1996 (b).

Sulamī, A. ʿA. R. (al-), *Haqāʾiq al-tafsīr*, Beirut, 2001, 2 vols.

———, *Ziyādat haqāʾiq al-tafsīr*, ed. G. Böwering, Beirut, 1986.

Suyūtī, J. D. (al-), *al-Hāwī li l-fatāwī*, Cairo, 1959, 2 vols.

———, *al-Durr al-manthūr*, Beirut, n.d., 6 vols.

Tabarī, M. b. J. (al-), *Jāmiʿ al-bayān fī tafsīr al-qurʾān*, Beirut, 1978, 12 vols.

———, *Mohammad, Sceau des prophètes*, trans. Zotenberg, Paris, 1980.

Tabarī, A. (al-), *Dhakhāʾir al-ʿuqbā fī manāqib dhawī l-qurbā*, ed. F. Bauden, Cairo, 2004.

Thaʾlabī, A. b. M. (al-), *Qisas al-anbiyāʾ al-musammā ʿarāʾis al-majālis*, Beirut, n.d.

Thomassen, E. and Radtke, B., *The Letters of Ahmad Ibn Idrīs*, London, 1993.

Tirmidhī, H. (al-), *K. Khatm al-awliyāʾ*, ed. O. Yahia, Beirut, 1965.

———, *K. Sīrat al-awliyāʾ*, ed. B. Radtke in *Thalātha musannafāt li l-Hakīm Tirmidhī*, Beirut, 1992.

———, *Manāzil al-qurba*, ed., Khalid Zahrī, Rabat, 2002.

———, *Nawādir al-usūl*, Beirut, 1992, 2 vols.

Tustarī, S. (al-), *Tafsīr al-qurʾān al-ʿazīm*, Beirut, 2002.

Vâlsan, M., "L'investiture du cheikh al-akbar au centre suprême", in *Études traditionnelles*, num. 311, Oct.-Nov. 1953, pp. 300-311.

Vikør, K. S., *Sufi and Scholar on the Desert Edge*, London, 1995.

Vimercati Sanseverino, R., "Fès et sainteté (808-1912), hagiographie, tradition spirituelle et héritage prophétique," doctoral thesis, Aix-Marseille, January, 2012.

Von Schlegell, B., "Sufism in the Ottoman Arab World: Shaykh 'Abd al-Ghanī al-Nābulusī (d. 1143/1731)," doctoral thesis, University of California at Berkeley, 1977.

Wāsitī, A. (al-), *al-Sulūk wa l-sayr ilā Llāh*, ms., Damascus, num. 4709, folios 1-148.

Watt, W. M. "The Authenticity of the Works Attributed to al-Ghazālī", in *Journal of the Royal Asiatic Society*, vol. LXXXIV, num. 1-2, 1952, pp. 24-45.

Wensinck, A. J., *Concordance et indices de la tradition musulmane*, Leiden, 1947, 6 vols.

Yahia, O., *Histoire et classification de l'œuvre d'Ibn 'Arabī*, Damascus, 1964, 2 vols.

Zabīdī M. (al-), *'Iqd al-jawhar al-thamīn*, ms. from the private collection of M. Riyād al-Mālih.

———, *Ithāf al-asfiyā'*, ms., in *ibid*.

Ziriklī, K. D. (al-), *al-A'lām*, Beirut, 1984, 8 vols.

Zurqānī, Y. (al-), *Sharh al-mawāhib al-laduniyya bi l-minah al-muhammadiyya*, Beirut, 1996, 12 vols.

Index